# A Human Rights-Based Approach to
# EDUCATION FOR ALL

**A framework for the realization
of children's right to education
and rights within education**

United Nations
Educational, Scientific and
Cultural Organization

# CONTENTS

# PREFACE AND ACKNOWLEDGEMENTS

This document brings together the current thinking and practice on human rights-based approaches in the education sector. It presents key issues and challenges in rights-based approaches and provides a framework for policy and programme development from the level of the school up to the national and international levels.

Rights-based approaches have only recently become a focus within the education sector. This document was thus developed as a resource for government officials, civil society organizations, United Nations and bilateral agencies, and other development partners strategically involved in the development of education policies and programmes. It is intended to guide the dialogue of the United Nations Development Group and Education for All (EFA) partnerships and facilitate a breakthrough from the rhetoric of the 'right to education' to concrete and accelerated interventions at policy and programme levels for attaining the EFA goals and the Millennium Development Goals related to education.

The document is positioned within and builds on the UN Statement of Common Understanding on a Human Rights-Based Approach to Development Cooperation. In this regard we hope it will be shared and used within the context of UN Reform and donor harmonization. More particularly, we hope it will be adopted by the UN Education Theme Group at the country level in developing the education component of a Common Country Assessment/UN Development Assistance Framework and to guide a common UN stance in larger country-level forums, such as education sector-wide approaches, the Multi-Donor Budget Support Group, the EFA Fast Track Initiative, the EFA Group, the Consultative Group and others.

While the predominant focus of the document is on primary basic education and child rights within education, it is based on the EFA goals and situated within life-cycle and lifelong learning approaches. It addresses the right *to* education as well as rights *within* education, which include human rights education itself. The document therefore needs also to be seen in the context of the World Programme for Human Rights Education, which was adopted through a UN General Assembly resolution in 2004, and which is being implemented through a Plan of Action, prepared by the Office of the United Nations High Commissioner for Human Rights (OHCHR) and the United Nations Educational, Scientific and Cultural Organization (UNESCO), with a focus on primary and secondary school systems in its first phase.

The project of preparing this document was initially started by the United Nations Children's Fund (UNICEF) (as a collaborative initiative between its Education Section and Human Rights Unit) and evolved as a joint effort with UNESCO. It draws on a participatory process that included a community of human rights education professionals, who, at different points in time – and from their diverse institutional, regional and thematic perspectives – have contributed actively through a number of meetings, consultations and discussions between 2004 and 2006.

One such meeting was held by UNESCO in Belfast in 2004, organized by the Section of Education for Peace and Human Rights and the University of Ulster, which hosts the UNESCO Chair in Education for Pluralism, Human Rights and Democracy. The recommendations from this meeting identified the need for guidance material on the application of a rights-based approach that is specific to the education sector and responds to the UN Statement of Common Understanding. The view was put strongly that the concept of 'quality' goes beyond physical inputs to and academic outputs from education, and includes educational content and processes that are consistent with human rights principles and practices.

A further stage involved the development of some basic planning tools – essentially checklists related to access, inclusion and quality. For this step, UNESCO Bangkok convened a meeting of national EFA Coordinators from Cambodia, the Lao People's Democratic Republic, Thailand and Viet Nam to pilot and comment on these instruments. The results led to further in-country meetings in 2005 to raise awareness of a rights-based approach to education among education ministry officials. The workshops drew heavily on the *Manual on Rights-Based Education,* by Katarina Tomaševski, former UN Special Rapporteur on the Right to Education (1998–2004).[1]

Simultaneously, UNICEF was receiving support from the Department for International Development (DFID), United Kingdom, for an ongoing project by its Human Rights Unit on 'Strengthening Human Rights-Based Approach Programming in UNICEF'. Five country case studies on the rights-based approach to education (Bolivia, Burkina Faso, Chile, Eritrea and Liberia) were developed as part of this project and underlined the need for technical guidance on the issue. A workshop was subsequently organized by UNICEF's Education Section in Panama in November 2005 and rallied UNICEF colleagues from the Americas and the Caribbean and Asia, together with representatives from human rights institutions and UNESCO. The Panama debates translated the richness and complexities of the rights-based approach into the first draft of this framework, and the Panama participants recommended a joint production with UNESCO. This collaboration was formalized in ensuing discussions between the two agencies.

In 2006, a global consultation, convened by both UNICEF and UNESCO and hosted by the Innocenti Research Centre, took place in Florence. Participants included UNICEF and UNESCO colleagues (from four regions and from different functions, including Representatives and education officers), multilateral agencies (the Organisation for Economic Co-operation and Development, the United Nations Development Programme and the World Bank), civil society organizations (Save the Children and the African Network Campaign on EFA), government representatives (Professor George Godia from the Kenyan Ministry of Education and Cristián Bellei, a former adviser to the Government of Chile), and the UNESCO Chair in Education for Pluralism, Human Rights and Democracy. The purpose was to revise the final draft of the document and to develop a broad understanding, consensus and 'buy-in' around it.

The Florence participants expressed their appreciation of the participatory process and of the opportunity to dialogue around and contribute to the development of a document that reflects the perspective of diverse stakeholders. Government representatives highlighted the complexities of the exercise and actually gave more concrete meaning to it in terms of relevance to countries. Civil society organizations insisted that the endorsement of the document by bilateral and multilateral agencies would immensely facilitate their work. The effort of capturing the different and competing views, of weaving in tensions, and of engaging the mandates and different perspectives was challenging, while at the same time it enriched the content of the framework.

The present document was principally drafted by Gerison Lansdown, an international expert contracted by UNICEF. Ms Lansdown was the founder and director, in 1992, of the Children's Rights Alliance for England, established to promote implementation of the United Nations Convention on the Rights of the Child. She has published and lectured widely on the subject of children's rights. Her unrelenting efforts at capturing and integrating the diverse inputs throughout the consultation process went beyond her mandate, and her engagement has been highly appreciated.

An editorial UNICEF/UNESCO team was formed for supporting the international expert in finalizing the document. It was composed of (in alphabetical order): Mialy Clark (consultant, UNESCO), Dina Craissati (Senior Adviser, Education, UNICEF HQ), Upala Devi Banerjee (Asia-Pacific Regional Coordinator, United Nations Inter-Agency Lessons Learned Project on the Human Rights-Based Approach to Development), Jessica Drohan (consultant, UNESCO), Paolo Fontani (Programme Manager, Education, UNESCO Office for the Caribbean), Linda King (Chief, Section for the Promotion of Rights and Values in Education, UNESCO), Garren Lumpkin (Regional

Education Adviser, UNICEF The Americas and Caribbean Regional Office), Dorothy Rozga (Deputy Regional Director, UNICEF East and Southern Africa Regional Office), Kishore Singh (Programme Specialist, UNESCO) and Alan Smith (UNESCO Chair in Education for Human Rights, Pluralism and Democracy).

The limited space here does not allow for thanks to be extended individually to all those who have contributed in one way or another to make this document a reality. The participants in the diverse meetings have not only shown exceptional engagement but also added greatly to its quality. Particular thanks go to (in alphabetical order): Gbemisola Akinboyo (UNICEF), Akila Belembeago (UNICEF), Egidio Crotti (UNICEF), Emilie Filmer-Wilson (UNDP), Stuart Hart (International Institute for Child Rights and Development), Bernard Hugonnier (OECD), Peter Hyll-Larsen (UNESCO), Victor Karunan (UNICEF), Nils Kastberg (UNICEF), Johan Lindeberg (UNESCO), Kathleen Moriarty (Save the Children UK), Lakshmi Narasimhan Balaji (UNICEF), David Parker (UNICEF), Mahesh Patel (UNICEF), Robert Prouty (World Bank), Olof Sandkull (UNESCO), Marta Santos Pais (UNICEF) and Linda Tinio (UNESCO).

The project was coordinated by Dina Craissati and Linda King.

We hope that the remarkable commitment demonstrated in producing the present framework will now be continued at global, regional and country levels in terms of policy dialogues and partnership building, programme reforms and development interventions.

**Cream Wright**
**Global Chief of Education**
**United Nations Children's Fund**

**Ann Therese Ndong-Jatta**
**Director, Division for the Promotion of**
**Basic Education**
**United Nations Educational, Scientific**
**and Cultural Organization**

# FOREWORD

At the 2000 World Education Forum held in Dakar (Senegal), the international community reaffirmed its commitment to achieving Education for All, a movement introduced 10 years earlier at the World Conference on Education for All, held in Jomtien (Thailand). Participants also adopted the Dakar Framework for Action and identified six specific goals:

- Expand early childhood care and education.
- Provide free and compulsory primary education for all.
- Promote learning and life skills for young people and adults.
- Increase adult literacy by 50 per cent, especially for women.
- Achieve gender parity by 2005 and gender equality by 2015.
- Improve the quality of education.

Underlying each of these goals is recognition of and respect for the right to quality education. Full realization of the right to education is not merely a question of access. A rights-based approach to Education for All is a holistic one, encompassing access to education, educational quality (based on human rights values and principles) and the environment in which education is provided. This document provides a framework for implementing and ensuring such an approach.

While the right to education – like all human rights – is universal and inalienable, several conventions have enshrined it in international law, thereby placing binding commitments on ratifying States. Provisions on the right to a quality education inclusive of human rights values appear in such treaties as the United Nations Educational, Scientific and Cultural Organization's Convention against Discrimination in Education (1960), the International Covenant on Economic, Social and Cultural Rights (1966) and the United Nations Convention on the Rights of the Child (1989).

In its General Comment No. 1, the Committee on the Rights of the Child provides further insight into the aims of education under Article 29 of the Convention on the Rights of the Child.[2] The Committee highlights the holistic nature of the right to education and, as the Committee on Economic, Social and Cultural Rights does in its General Comment No. 13,[3] underscores the role of education in empowering individuals.

The Education for All movement is, as its name suggests, directed towards all people: children, youth and adults. The Convention on the Rights of the Child highlights the particular significance of education for young people, and this document focuses primarily on the educational rights of children. But the right to education has no age limit. Additionally, Education for All emphasizes the need to provide access to education for traditionally marginalized groups, including girls and women, indigenous populations and remote rural groups, street children, migrants and nomadic populations, people with disabilities, and linguistic and cultural minorities. A comprehensive rights-based approach must be dynamic, accounting for different learning environments and different learners.

Each of the instruments named above illustrates the importance of a rights-based approach to education. However, without effective implementation, they remain only that – illustrations, ideas and conceptions of what a rights-friendly learning environment could be. This document acknowledges that a rights-based approach to education is not without its obstacles. Nevertheless, a sustainable human rights-based approach can be attained if key players fulfil their existing commitments and work towards further progress.

Education is not a static commodity to be considered in isolation from its greater context; it is an ongoing process and holds its own inherent value as a human right. Not only do people have the right to receive quality education now, they also have the right to be equipped with the skills and knowledge that will ensure long-term recognition of and respect for all human rights. As the Committee on Economic, Social and Cultural Rights observes in the opening lines of its General Comment No. 13, "… education is the primary vehicle by which economically and socially marginalized adults and children can lift themselves out of poverty and obtain the means to participate fully in their communities."[4]

Thus, a rights-based approach to education is imperative. Schooling that is respectful of human rights – both in words and in action, in schoolbooks and the schoolyard – is integral to the realization of quality education for all. Complex barriers can impede the goals of Education for All; a rights-based approach to education plays a key role in overcoming such obstacles. The following pages elaborate an overarching policy and programming framework for achieving quality education that is in keeping with human rights norms and values, and is truly Education for All.

**Vernor Muñoz**
**United Nations Special Rapporteur on the Right to Education**

# ACRONYMS

| | |
|---|---|
| **CCA** | Common Country Assessment |
| **CESCR** | Committee on Economic, Social and Cultural Rights |
| **CRC** | Convention on the Rights of the Child |
| **EFA** | Education for All |
| **ILO** | International Labour Organization |
| **INEE** | Inter-Agency Network for Education in Emergencies |
| **NGO** | non-governmental organization |
| **OECD** | Organisation for Economic Co-operation and Development |
| **OHCHR** | Office of the United Nations High Commissioner for Human Rights |
| **SWAps** | sector-wide approaches |
| **UDHR** | Universal Declaration of Human Rights |
| **UN** | United Nations |
| **UNAIDS** | Joint United Nations Programme on HIV/AIDS |
| **UNDAF** | United Nations Development Assistance Framework |
| **UNDP** | United Nations Development Programme |
| **UNESCO** | United Nations Educational, Scientific and Cultural Organization |
| **UNFPA** | United Nations Population Fund |
| **UNGEI** | United Nations Girls Education Initiative |
| **UNHCR** | United Nations High Commissioner for Refugees |
| **UNICEF** | United Nations Children's Fund |
| **UNRWA** | United Nations Relief and Works Agency for Palestine Refugees in the Near East |
| **USAID** | United States Agency for International Development |

# *My right to learn*

**By Robert Prouty**

*I do not have to earn*
*The right to learn.*
*It's mine.*
*And if because*
*Of faulty laws*
*And errors of design,*
*And far too many places where*
*Still far too many people do not care –*
*If because of all these things, and more,*
*For me, the classroom door,*
*With someone who can teach,*
*Is still beyond my reach,*
*Still out of sight,*
*Those wrongs do not remove my right.*

*So here I am. I too*
*Am one of you*
*And by God's grace,*
*And yours, I'll find my place.*

*We haven't met.*
*You do not know me yet*
*And so*
*You don't yet know*
*That there is much that I can give you in return.*
*The future is my name*
*And all I claim*
*Is this: my right to learn.*

# INTRODUCTION

The goal of a human rights-based approach to education is simple: to assure every child a quality education that respects and promotes her or his right to dignity and optimum development. Achieving this goal is, however, enormously more complex.

The right to education is high on the agenda of the international community. It is affirmed in numerous human rights treaties and recognized by governments as pivotal in the pursuit of development and social transformation. This recognition is exemplified in the international goals, strategies and targets that have been set during the past 20 years. The Education for All goals were established at Jomtien (Thailand) in 1990 and reaffirmed at the 2000 World Education Forum in Dakar (Senegal). In the Millennium Development Goals, established in 2000, the world's governments committed to achieving universal access to free, quality and compulsory primary education by 2015. In 'A World Fit for Children', the outcome document from the United Nations General Assembly Special Session on Children in 2002, governments reaffirmed these commitments and agreed to a range of strategies and actions to achieve them. More ambitious targets have been established in many regions. Countries in Latin America and the Caribbean, for example, are increasingly making school attendance compulsory for children of pre-primary age.[5] These various strategies have had an effect: In 1948, when education was recognized as a human right, only a minority of the world's children had access to any formal education; now a majority of them go to school, and participation in formal education beyond the elementary stages has increased.

However, the progress made to date is far from adequate. UNESCO statistics on enrolment indicate that 77 million children in 2004 were still not enrolled in school. According to UNICEF sources this figure may be as high as 90 million children for 2005–2006 in terms of school attendance figures from household surveys.[6] In many regions, girls lag far behind. In other regions, there is a growing problem of underachievement by boys. Poverty is a key factor impeding enrolment, primary and secondary completion, and learning outcomes, and children from ethnic minority and indigenous communities consistently underachieve. The evidence indicates that, on current trajectories, the international targets for access will not be met. The challenges to the achievement of quality in education are even greater. Most international attention has been focused on helping children get into school. What happens once they are there, and the nature of the education they receive, has been afforded far less emphasis. As a consequence, even if they go to school, huge numbers of children experience a quality of education that is extremely poor, leaving them without the skills and knowledge they need to lift themselves out of poverty. The failure of such schooling to fulfil human rights is illustrated by national test data from a number of countries including Bangladesh, Brazil, Ghana, Pakistan, the Philippines and Zambia. These show a majority of primary school leavers to be achieving well below their countries' minimum performance standards, with results in some cases being "only marginally better than for children who have not completed school."[7]

Although there are notable and creative exceptions to the rule, there is growing recognition that the approaches adopted to achieve the goals of universal access and quality education are inadequate. There has been a failure to acknowledge the complexity of the barriers impeding children's access to school, to listen to the concerns expressed by children themselves concerning their education, to build a culture of education in which all children are equally respected and valued, to engage parents and local communities in supporting education, to embrace a holistic approach to education, to address children's rights in education or to embed schools as vibrant centres for community action and social development. Energy has been focused too narrowly on enrolment, without sufficient attention to attendance, completion and attainment, or to the processes through which those outcomes can be achieved.

Many international agencies have, therefore, increasingly turned to a human rights-based approach. As early as 1997, as part of the United Nations Programme for Reform, the UN Secretary-General called on all entities of the UN system to bring human rights into the mainstream of their activities and programmes. The outcome was the UN Statement of Common Understanding, which integrates international human rights into plans, strategies and policies associated with development programmes (*see Appendix I, page 113*). The rights-based approach focuses on the inalienable human rights of each individual, as expressed in UN instruments, and on governments' obligation to fulfil, respect and protect those internationally defined human rights. In so doing, it aims to support and empower individuals and communities to claim their rights. In addition, a distinctive feature of this approach is that it requires an equal commitment to both process and outcomes.

Adopting a rights-based approach to education is not a panacea. It does pose some challenges – for example, the need to balance the claims of different rights holders and address potential tensions between the realization of different rights or between rights and responsibilities. Nevertheless, consistent adherence to its core principles can help meet the education goals of governments, parents and children. It demands the creation of strategies to reach all children, including the most marginalized. It empowers communities, parents and other stakeholders to claim their rights, insist that these be fully implemented and, when necessary, seek their enforcement in national courts.

Many publications have been produced on the multiple aspects of Education for All, but there has been no comprehensive analysis of the actions necessary to undertake a rights-based approach to achieving its goals. This document is intended to fill that gap. It aims to provide readers with a conceptual analysis of the meaning and scope of a rights-based approach to education. It also offers a comprehensive framework of strategies and actions necessary to translate those human rights into legislation, policies and programmes for the attainment of Education for All. Together, the conceptual analysis and the framework can be used as a resource for advocacy and social mobilization. They provide the tools with which to conduct a critical review of the current state of education in any country from a human rights perspective and to engage in political dialogue with governments and other partners with a view to adopting a rights-based approach.

Given its intention to offer a framework, this publication does not and cannot provide detailed guidance for the implementation of rights-based programmes. Furthermore, it cannot address the specific and widely differing concerns faced in different countries or regions of the world. Obviously, the capacities of governments to fulfil their obligations in terms of education vary greatly. Armed conflict, AIDS, poverty, natural disasters, internal displacement, corruption and weak government all have a direct impact on education and the strategies needed to ensure it is provided for every child. Nor can this publication detail the complex and challenging strategies needed to target many of the most marginalized children. However, the overarching framework it provides has application in all contexts and can be used by all those involved in promoting the right to education. Stakeholders are encouraged to use it to develop programmes and activities for their specific social, economic and cultural context.

The predominant focus in this publication is on basic education, but within a life-cycle and lifelong learning approach. It uses the Education for All goals as a foundation, but addresses the educational rights of children rather than adults. Not only does it focus on the right to education, it also addresses rights within education, including human rights education. In so doing, it recognizes that there is an integral relationship between the obligations to fulfil, to respect and to protect rights, and that all are vitally important if the Education for All goals are to be achieved. Governments, with the active participation of civil society partners, have to fulfil their obligations to ensure the right to education and intensify their efforts to promote human rights education by the provision of quality learning environments for all children.

The publication is divided into four chapters:

**Chapter 1** provides a brief historical overview of the right to education, international commitments to its realization and key aspects of a rights-based approach to development. It also discusses applying this approach to education policy and programming, and looks at some of the tensions that may arise between different rights, among rights holders, and between rights and responsibilities.

**Chapter 2** introduces a conceptual framework for the rights-based approach to education that embodies three interlinked and interdependent dimensions. It contends that human rights related to education cannot be realized unless and until all three are addressed:

- **The right of access to education** – the right of every child to education on the basis of equality of opportunity and without discrimination on any grounds. To achieve this goal, education must be available for, accessible to and inclusive of all children.
- **The right to quality education** – the right of every child to a quality education that enables him or her to fulfil his or her potential, realize opportunities for employment and develop life skills. To achieve this goal, education needs to be child-centred, relevant and embrace a broad curriculum, and be appropriately resourced and monitored.
- **The right to respect within the learning environment** – the right of every child to respect for her or his inherent dignity and to have her or his universal human rights respected within the education system. To achieve this goal, education must be provided in a way that is consistent with human rights, including equal respect for every child, opportunities for meaningful participation, freedom from all forms of violence, and respect for language, culture and religion.

**Chapter 3** addresses state obligations. It identifies the importance of a supportive political and economic environment, a robust legislative framework and rights-based education policies if governments are to realize the Education for All goals, and it elaborates the actions needed in each of these three areas.

**Chapter 4** focuses on other stakeholders: parents and other caregivers, communities, teachers, civil society organizations and the international community. It explores the rights and responsibilities of these actors and the ways they can contribute to the realization of the right to education.

The text is illustrated by case examples from a variety of countries. Several appendices are also included to provide background information and elaborate on issues raised in the framework, including standards on child participation, human rights education, and international goals and commitments. In addition, there is a checklist of actions necessary to achieve a rights-based approach to education, and a bibliography of relevant documents, websites and initiatives.

# HUMAN RIGHTS AND EDUCATION

## EDUCATION AS A HUMAN RIGHT

Education has been formally recognized as a human right since the adoption of the Universal Declaration of Human Rights in 1948. This has since been affirmed in numerous global human rights treaties, including the United Nations Educational, Scientific and Cultural Organization (UNESCO) Convention against Discrimination in Education (1960), the International Covenant on Economic, Social and Cultural Rights (1966) and the Convention on the Elimination of All Forms of Discrimination against Women (1981). These treaties establish an entitlement to free, compulsory primary education for all children; an obligation to develop secondary education, supported by measures to render it accessible to all children, as well as equitable access to higher education; and a responsibility to provide basic education for individuals who have not completed primary education. Furthermore, they affirm that the aim of education is to promote personal development, strengthen respect for human rights and freedoms, enable individuals to participate effectively in a free society, and promote understanding, friendship and tolerance. The right to education has long been recognized as encompassing not only access to educational provision, but also the obligation to eliminate discrimination at all levels of the educational system, to set minimum standards and to improve quality. In addition, education is necessary for the fulfilment of any other civil, political, economic or social right.

The United Nations Convention on the Rights of the Child (1989) further strengthens and broadens the concept of the right to education, in particular through the obligation to consider in its implementation the Convention's four core principles: non-discrimination; the best interests of the child; the right to life, survival and development of the child to the maximum extent possible; and the right of children to express their views in all matters affecting them and for their views to be given due weight in accordance with their age and maturity[8] (*see Appendix II, page 118*). These underlying principles make clear a strong commitment to ensuring that children are recognized as active agents in their own learning and that education is designed to promote and respect their rights and needs. The Convention elaborates an understanding of the right to education in terms of universality, participation, respect and inclusion. This approach is exemplified both in the text itself and in its interpretation by the Committee on the Rights of the Child, the international body established to monitor governments' progress in implementing child rights.

## Perspectives introduced in the Convention on the Rights of the Child

- The right to education is to be achieved on the basis of equality of opportunity.

- Measures must be taken to encourage regular school attendance and reduce dropout. It is not sufficient just to provide formal education. It is also necessary to remove such barriers as poverty and discrimination and to provide education of sufficient quality, in a manner that ensures children can benefit from it.

- Discipline must be administered in a manner consistent both with the child's dignity and with the right to protection from all forms of violence, thus sustaining respect for the child in the educational environment.

- The aims of education are defined in terms of the potential of each child and the scope of the curriculum, clearly establishing that education should be a preparatory process for promoting and respecting human rights. This approach is elaborated in the General Comment on the aims of education, in which the Committee on the Rights of the Child stresses that article 29 requires the development of education that is child centred, child friendly and empowering, and that education goes beyond formal schooling to embrace a broad range of life experiences through which positive development and learning occur.

- In its General Comment on early childhood, the Committee on the Rights of the Child interprets the right to education as beginning at birth and encourages governments to take measures and provide programmes to enhance parental capacities to promote their children's development.

**Sources:** United Nations Convention on the Rights of the Child, 1989; Committee on the Rights of the Child, 'General Comment No. 1: The aims of education, article 29 (1) (2001)', CRC/GC/2001/1, 2001; Committee on the Rights of the Child, 'General Comment No. 7: Implementing child rights in early childhood', CRC/C/GC7, 2005.

Beyond the formal obligations undertaken by governments in ratifying these human rights treaties, a number of global conferences have affirmed the right to education. Although lacking the legally binding force of the treaties, these conferences have introduced an additional impetus for action, together with elaborated commitments and time frames for their attainment. The World Conference on Education for All (1990) set the goal of universal primary education for the year 2000, a goal not met but subsequently reaffirmed for 2015 at the World Education Forum in 2000. This Forum also committed to an expansion and improvement of early childhood care and education, the elimination of gender disparities in education and the improvement of quality in education.

In addition, the international community and leading development institutions have agreed to the Millennium Development Goals, expressed in the Millennium Declaration, which commit them to ensuring that all girls and boys complete a full course of primary education and that gender disparity is eliminated at all levels of education by 2015 (*see Appendix III, page 120*). More recently, the 'International Conference on the Right to Basic Education as a Fundamental Human Right and the Legal Framework for Its Financing' (Jakarta, Indonesia, 2–4 December 2005) adopted the Jakarta Declaration. This emphasizes that the right to education is an internationally recognized right in its interrelationship with the right to development, and that the legal and constitutional protection of this right is indispensable to its full realization.

## HUMAN RIGHTS-BASED APPROACHES TO DEVELOPMENT

An increasing emphasis has been placed in recent years on rights-based approaches to development. In part, this shift has been the result of growing recognition that needs-based or service-delivery approaches have failed to substantially reduce poverty. One significant limitation of these approaches has been that they are often undertaken by authorities who may not be sensitive to the needs of the poor. It is also felt that combining human rights, development and activism can be more effective than any single approach.

As part of the UN Programme for Reform launched in 1997, the UN Secretary-General called on all entities of the UN system to mainstream human rights into their activities and programmes. This led to an inter-agency process of negotiation, resulting in the adoption of a UN Statement of Common Understanding that has been accepted by the UN Development Group (*see Appendix I, page 113*). The statement provides a conceptual, analytical and methodological framework for identifying, planning, designing and monitoring development activities based on international human rights standards. Essentially, it integrates the norms, standards and principles of international human rights into the entire process of development programming, including plans, strategies and policies. It seeks to create greater awareness among governments and other relevant institutions of their obligations to fulfil, respect and protect human rights and to support and empower individuals and communities to claim their rights.

## The principles that inform a rights-based approach

- **Universality and inalienability:** Human rights are universal and inalienable, the entitlement of all people everywhere in the world. An individual cannot voluntarily give them up. Nor can others take them away. As stated in article 1 of the Universal Declaration of Human Rights, "All human beings are born free and equal in dignity and rights."
- **Indivisibility:** Human rights are indivisible. Whether civil, cultural, economic, political or social, they are all inherent to the dignity of every person. Consequently, they all have equal status as rights and cannot be ranked in a hierarchy.
- **Interdependence and interrelatedness:** The realization of one right often depends, wholly or in part, on the realization of others. For example, realization of the right to health may depend on realization of the right to information.
- **Equality and non-discrimination:** All individuals are equal as human beings, and by virtue of the inherent dignity of each person, are entitled to their rights without discrimination of any kind. A rights-based approach requires a particular focus on addressing discrimination and inequality. Safeguards need to be included in development instruments to protect the rights and well-being of marginalized groups. As far as possible, data need to be disaggregated – for example, by sex, religion, ethnicity, language and disability – in order to give visibility to potentially vulnerable populations. Furthermore, all development decisions, policies and initiatives, while seeking to empower local participants, are also expressly required to guard against reinforcing power imbalances or contributing to the creation of new ones.
- **Participation and inclusion:** Every person and all peoples are entitled to active, free and meaningful participation in, contribution to and enjoyment of civil, economic, social, cultural and political development, through which human rights and fundamental freedoms can be enjoyed.
- **Empowerment:** Empowerment is the process by which people's capabilities to demand and use their human rights grow. They are empowered to claim

their rights rather than simply wait for policies, legislation or the provision of services. Initiatives should be focused on building the capacities of individuals and communities to hold those responsible to account. The goal is to give people the power and capabilities to change their own lives, improve their own communities and influence their own destinies.

- **Accountability and respect for the rule of law:** A rights-based approach seeks to raise levels of accountability in the development process by identifying 'rights holders' and corresponding 'duty bearers' and to enhance the capacities of those duty bearers to meet their obligations. These include both positive obligations to protect, promote and fulfil human rights, as well as negative obligations to abstain from rights violations. In addition to governments, a wide range of other actors should also carry responsibilities for the realization of human rights, including individuals, local organizations and authorities, the private sector, the media, donors, development partners and international institutions. The international community also carries obligations to provide effective cooperation in response to the shortages of resources and capacities in developing countries. A rights-based approach requires the development of laws, administrative procedures, and practices and mechanisms to ensure the fulfilment of entitlements, as well as opportunities to address denials and violations. It also calls for the translation of universal standards into locally determined benchmarks for measuring progress and enhancing accountability.

## ADOPTING A RIGHTS-BASED APPROACH TO EDUCATION

Needs-based development approaches to education have, to date, failed to achieve the Education for All goals. Because it is inclusive and provides a common language for partnership, a rights-based approach – although certainly not without tensions and challenges – has the potential to contribute to the attainment of the goals of governments, parents and children. Girls' right to education, for example, can be achieved more effectively if measures are also implemented to address their rights to freedom from discrimination, protection from exploitative labour, physical violence and sexual abuse, and access to an adequate standard of living.[9] Equally, the right to education is instrumental in the realization of other rights. Research indicates, for example, that one additional year of schooling for 1,000 women helps prevent two maternal deaths.[10]

A rights-based approach can contribute significant added value:

- **It promotes social cohesion, integration and stability:** Human rights promote democracy and social progress. Even where children have access to school, a poor quality of education can contribute to disaffection. A rights-based approach to education, which emphasizes quality, can encourage the development of school environments in which children know their views are valued. It includes a focus on respect for families and the values of the society in which they are living. It can also promote understanding of other cultures and peoples, contributing to intercultural dialogue and respect for the richness of cultural and linguistic diversity, and the right to participate in cultural life. In this way, it can serve to strengthen social cohesion.
- **It builds respect for peace and non-violent conflict resolution:** A rights-based approach to education is founded on principles of peace and non-violent conflict resolution. In achieving this goal, schools and communities must create learning environments that eliminate all forms of physical, sexual or humiliating punishment by teachers and challenge all forms of bullying and aggression among students. In other words, they must promote and build a culture of non-violent conflict resolution. The lessons children learn from school-based experiences in this regard can have far-reaching consequences for the wider society.
- **It contributes to positive social transformation:** A rights-based approach to education that embodies human rights education empowers children and other stakeholders and represents a major building block in efforts to achieve social transformation towards rights-respecting societies and social justice.
- **It is more cost-effective and sustainable:** Treating children with dignity and respect – and building inclusive, participatory and accountable education systems that respond directly to the expressed concerns of all stakeholders – will serve to improve educational outcomes. In too many schools, the failure to adapt to the needs of children, particularly working children, results in high levels of dropout and repeated grades. Children themselves cite violence and abuse, discriminatory attitudes, an irrelevant curriculum and poor teaching quality as major contributory factors in the inability to learn effectively and in subsequent dropout.[11] In addition, health issues can diminish the ability of a child to commence and continue schooling, and for all children, especially girls, an inclusive education can reduce the risk of HIV infection.[12] A rights-based approach is therefore not only cost-effective and economically beneficial but also more sustainable.
- **It produces better outcomes for economic development:** A rights-based approach to education can be entirely consistent with the broader agenda

of governments to produce an economically viable workforce. Measures to promote universal access to education and overcome discrimination against girls, children with disabilities, working children, children in rural communities, and minority and indigenous children will serve to widen the economic base of society, thus strengthening a country's economic capability.

- **It builds capacity:** By focusing on capacity-building and empowerment, a rights-based approach to education harnesses and develops the capacities of governments to fulfil their obligations and of individuals to claim their rights and entitlements.

## APPLYING A RIGHTS-BASED APPROACH TO POLICY AND PROGRAMMING

The UN Statement of Common Understanding elaborates what is understood to be a rights-based approach to development cooperation and development programming. It emphasizes that all programmes of development cooperation, policies and technical assistance should further the realization of human rights, and therefore that human rights principles and standards should guide all phases of the programming process. The following elements are necessary, specific and unique to a rights-based approach and can be used for policy and programming in the education sector:

- Assessment and analysis identify the claims of human rights in education and the corresponding obligations of governments, as well as the immediate, underlying and structural causes of the non-realization of rights.
- Programmes assess the capacity of individuals to claim their rights and of governments to fulfil their obligations. Strategies are then developed to build those capacities.
- Programmes monitor and evaluate both the outcomes and processes, guided by human rights standards and principles.
- Programming is informed by the recommendations of international human rights bodies and mechanisms.

In addition, many elements of good programming practice are essential within a rights-based approach. Overall, then, the required steps are:

- Situation assessment and analysis.
- Assessing capacity for implementation.
- Programme planning, design and implementation.
- Monitoring and evaluation.

## How 'good programming' can be enhanced

- In good programming, it is recognized that people cannot be developed; they must develop themselves. Children, young people and other learners, including those who are poor, should be recognized as key actors in their own education and development rather than as passive beneficiaries of services and transfers of commodities.

*In a rights-based approach to education, children and other learners, including those who are poor, are subjects of rights with 'claims to' education and 'claims from' duty bearers. Rights-based education programming should therefore develop the capacities of children, young people, their parents and other learners to claim their rights. Human rights education is an important instrument in empowering people to understand, claim and realize their rights.*

- In good programming, participation is crucial, both as an end and a means. Participation does not mean that 'they' participate in 'our' education programme, but rather that we all participate in meeting the learning needs identified.

*Participation, including children's and women's participation, is a human right enshrined in many conventions. In a rights-based approach to education, participation is both a necessary process and an outcome.*

- In good programming, empowerment is important, but it is not a strategy. Empowerment may be an aspect of any strategy, such as advocacy, capacity-building or service delivery.

*A rights-based approach, which implies dignity and respect for the individual, acknowledges that empowerment is both a necessary strategy and a goal. Emphasis is placed on promoting opportunities to obtain remedies for grievances through both formal and informal justice mechanisms.*

- In good programming, monitoring of outcome and processes, as well as actual use of information for decision-making at all levels of education, is very important.

*A rights-based approach implies accountability of those with duties or obligations in fulfilling, respecting and protecting the right to education.*

- In good programming, stakeholder analysis is very useful for the development and evaluation of education programmes because it identifies clear accountabilities in the community and society.

*Most stakeholders in education are also duty bearers. An important step in a rights-based approach is to identify the key relations between claim-holders and duty bearers. This is similar to, but goes beyond, stakeholder analysis.*

## by a human rights-based approach

*The relationship between claims and duties implies clear accountabilities – the commitments made under human rights treaties are entitlements, not promises or charity. Development assistance must be the result of those international obligations.*

- **In good programming, education programmes should respond to basic needs of children and other people, with a focus on vulnerable groups. Local ownership is important, and development support from outside should always build on existing capabilities. Poverty elimination and disparity reduction should be long-term goals in all education development efforts.**

*Education programmes should respond to need but must also take account of the rights of children, young people and other learners. Stakeholders in education should have an ownership of education programmes as a right, rather than an option. The right to education is a means to reduce disparity and poverty. Education programming should therefore articulate the explicit linkages between proposed actions and their relationship to reducing disparities and eliminating poverty and injustice. This may involve both institutional and legal reform. Human rights standards provide tools and legitimacy for advocacy for change.*

- **In good programming, education programmes should be developed on the basis of a situation analysis that identifies priority problems and their immediate, underlying and basic causes, which should be addressed either simultaneously or in sequence.**

*A rights-based approach to education requires that underlying causes of poverty and inequality be addressed. The indivisibility of human rights also emphasizes simultaneous attention to causes at all levels.*

- **In good programming, setting goals is important, and the necessity for scaling up should be considered at the planning stage. Efforts should be made to ensure that positive changes are sustainable and sustained. This includes environmental sustainability.**

*The realization of rights-based education requires both the achievement of desirable outcomes and achieving them through a process that reflects human rights values. A rights-based approach to education calls for simultaneous attention to outcomes and processes. A shift of focus is needed away from service delivery towards capacity development and advocacy.*

**Source:** Adapted from Jonsson, Urban, *A Human Rights Approach to Development Programming*, United Nations Children's Fund, New York, 2003, pp. 39–41.

## Situation assessment and analysis

Whereas a development approach to situation analysis addresses risks, power, stakeholders, root causes and gender, a rights-based approach to programming is informed by reference to the full range of relevant human rights – including any guidance provided by treaty bodies through General Comments and their concluding observations in relation to education. It also necessitates the following dimensions:[13]

- **Analysis of the legislative, policy and practice environment:** It is not sufficient that legislation is in place. Too often, legislation exists but is not implemented. Inadequate resources, lack of capacities in terms of the wherewithal to implement policy, lack of public demand and low levels of information, awareness and training render it ineffective, and there are no means of redress if the rights it introduces are not respected.
- **A focus on primary responsibility of governments:** In education, governments bear the primary responsibility to, for example, provide schools, train teachers, develop the curriculum, monitor standards, eliminate discrimination and promote equal opportunity of access. Other key players – such as local authorities, schools, parents and communities – also have responsibilities, although in some cases their capacities to fulfil these are necessarily dependent on the government meeting its primary responsibilities.
- **Applying the four central principles of the Convention on the Rights of the Child:** Non-discrimination, best interests of the child, the right to life, survival and development, and the right to express views and have them given due weight must be a focus throughout the analysis.
- **Analysis of rights violations and denials:** It is essential that this analysis includes the immediate, underlying and structural causes of violations and is extended to access to education, quality in education and respect for children's rights within education.
- **A focus on the poorest and most vulnerable:** These groups are usually the most disempowered and at greatest risk of violation or denial of their rights.
- **A participatory approach:** This enables the input of a range of stakeholders – including parents, teachers, religious leaders, community groups and children – into the analysis and provides opportunities to feed back on its conclusions. Children's perspectives are indispensable. Whenever possible, the views of girls and boys of different ages, in and out of school, with and without disabilities, and from different ethnic groups, geographic locations and socio-economic situations should be taken into account.

- **Disaggregated data:** To ensure the visibility of all groups of children in relation to enrolment, attendance, completion, attainment in education and other pertinent factors, it is crucial that data are disaggregated by sex, disability, race, ethnic or social origin, economic status, religion, language, geographic location and other status.

## Assessing capacity for implementation

A rights-based approach to education policy and programming places a particular focus on assessing the capacity of both rights holders to claim their rights and governments and public authorities to fulfil their obligations. The process should involve plans and activities to increase the capacity of individuals to support the implementation of education priorities.

### Capacities of rights holders to claim rights

In order to claim rights, people need to know what their rights are and how they are being addressed, how decisions are made and by whom, and what mechanisms, if any, exist to seek redress in cases of violations. If teachers are persistently absent or fail to teach, parents and the community need to know that their children have the right to education and that they should join together to demand the resolution of such problems. They need opportunities for access to policymakers and the media. They may also need support in analysing how their rights are being denied and how to argue their case for change. Efforts also need to be made to build opportunities for children to claim their rights. There is a growing body of tools and strategies for promoting children's access to the media, policymakers and politicians, as well as evidence of the capacity for effective child advocacy (*see Bibliography, page 102*). Empowering rights holders to claim their rights requires a range of strategies, including information, advocacy, capacity-building, parent networking, peer support and technical assistance.

### Capacities of government and public authorities to fulfil obligations

Assessment of the capacities of government and public authorities to meet their obligations with regard to educational rights is key. Obstacles to complying with responsibilities may derive from:

- **Lack of resources** – financial (tax base or budget priorities) or human (skills and institutional capacity).
- **Lack of authority** – legal, moral, spiritual or cultural.

- **Lack of responsibility** – refusing to accept obligations and demonstrating no political commitment to doing so.
- **Lack of coordination between levels and sectors.**
- **Lack of knowledge** – for example, illiterate parents may not know that they have an obligation to send their children to school.

The analysis will indicate the strategies necessary to achieve change. For example, in order to assess parents' capacities to fulfil their obligation to send their children to school, States need to analyse the real costs associated with schooling. The absence of school fees may be insufficient to eliminate the economic burden on parents; school uniforms, equipment and transportation, as well as the loss of domestic support or the earnings of a child, need to be included in the analysis when developing policies aimed at universal education. In situations of crisis, conflict and transition, the obstacles are likely to be particularly acute. However, it is possible to build capacity and commitment to sustain or restore access to education even in war-torn environments.

## Programme planning, design and implementation

A rights-based approach to programming recognizes that the process of development is as important as the outcome. Indeed, the process largely determines the type of outcome resulting from development activities. The principles that inform a rights-based approach outlined above (*page 10*) should be taken into consideration in the planning, design and implementation of programmes. Although not all are new to development practice – participation and accountability, for example, are also characteristic of good programming – the added value of a rights-based approach is that such principles acquire moral and political force.[14] This is important, given that the people who may benefit the most from the application of these principles, i.e., poor and marginalized groups, are not generally in a position to claim their rights.

Taking a rights-based approach to education will necessitate that:

- The programme engages with government in a constructive dialogue regarding its obligations, and how best it can fulfil these. This may require incentives and technical assistance, as well as capacity-building.
- Claims holders are involved in the assessment, decision-making and implementation of education provision.
- Evidence-based advocacy is used to increase the scale of impact through, for example, replication, legislative and policy change, and resource allocation.

- Civil society is involved in programme design and implementation to promote government accountability.
- Special attention is paid to the most marginalized and discriminated against groups. This approach involves going beyond addressing poorer communities to identify the most vulnerable people among the poor, for example, children with disabilities, children in low castes, internally displaced persons and children living with HIV. It then develops programming specifically to reach them.
- All programme activities are explicitly linked to human rights standards. Such standards set minimum guarantees for poor and disadvantaged groups. They also help identify where problems exist and what capacities and functions are required to address them. In the programming process, human rights standards can help define a comprehensive but targeted scope for development strategies that will yield more cost-effective results. They can also help to set results-based outcomes and outputs.

## Monitoring and evaluation

A rights-based approach to monitoring and evaluating education has implications, beyond those that would be addressed as good development practice, for both the process by which it is undertaken and the outcomes it seeks to measure.[15] In terms of process, there is a need for greater transparency of information about education provision. In addition, children and their communities need to be actively engaged as partners and involved in design, analysis, sharing of information and documentation. Their involvement empowers them and improves the quality of the information. Such monitoring and evaluation frameworks will help capture both the qualitative and quantitative indicators in respect of realizing the rights-based approach to education. In terms of outcomes, monitoring and evaluation needs to address:

- Changes in the lives of children to measure whether their education rights are better realized or no longer violated.
- Changes in legislation, policy, structures and practices and their impact on the realization of educational rights.
- Changes in relation to equity and non-discrimination in respect of access to education, the quality of that education and the experience of children within it. For example, have more marginalized children been reached and have discriminatory references in the curriculum been removed?
- Opportunities for participation and active citizenship of children, as well as other stakeholders, in schools and in the wider development of education policy.

- Changes in civil society and community capacity to support the rights-based approach – for example, through advocacy for improved education, active support for local schools, and ensuring the equal right of girls and boys. (*See Appendix IV, page 122.*)

# ADDRESSING TENSIONS IN FULFILLING THE RIGHT TO EDUCATION

A rights-based approach to programming is not a magic wand. It does not provide simple solutions to challenges that have proved intractable for many years. While providing a principled framework and a methodology for its application, it can also expose tensions, real or apparent, between different rights, among rights holders, and between rights and responsibilities.

## Reconciling conflicting agendas for education

In its General Comment on the aims of education, the Committee on the Rights of the Child emphasized that the overarching aim must be to promote, support and protect "the human dignity innate in every child and his or her equal and inalienable rights" while taking into account the child's developmental needs and diverse evolving capacities. This is to be achieved through the holistic development of the full potential of the child, including a respect for human rights, an enhanced sense of identity and affiliation, and socialization with others and with the environment.[16]

In practice, however, there are competing agendas for the aims of education systems. For governments, there are two major goals in funding education: to develop the economic workforce and potential future wealth; and to promote social cohesion, integration and a sense of national identity. Indeed, the development of mass education during the 20th century is recognized to have played an important role in promoting national integration and uniformity in both industrialized countries and the developing world.[17] A rights-based understanding of education moves beyond the more traditional model of schooling, which has defined the education agenda very much from the perspective of the government by emphasizing training, human capital investment, and containment of young people and their socialization.

Parents, too, have demands of the education system. Most parents want it to equip their children for a successful life, and hence expect it to provide their children with the knowledge, skills and confidence that will help them gain employment and achieve economic success. They also look to schools to transmit their values, culture and language – in other words, they seek in the education system the reinforcement and promotion of their own beliefs.

A third constituency with demands on education is, of course, the child, for whom the goal is acquiring the capacities through which to fulfil her or his aspirations. Education also provides the opportunity for emotional development and friendship outside the family. It is the route through which economically and socially marginalized children can escape poverty and participate fully in their communities. It also plays a vital role in safeguarding children from exploitative and hazardous labour and sexual exploitation, promoting human rights and democracy, and protecting the environment.[18]

There are, then, significant and sometimes competing expectations of the education system – from governments that are providing the legal and administrative framework and funding, from parents responsible for their children's upbringing and from children themselves as rights holders. Some expectations are common to all: economic success, reinforcement of values and social standing. However, the fact that governments are concerned with the wider society and parents with their individual child can and does create significant tensions in the education agenda. These tensions are acknowledged in international human rights law, which introduces the right of parents to educate their children according to their beliefs.[19] It reflects the need to limit a government's power to impose its economic, political and religious agenda on children.

The UN Convention on the Rights of the Child introduces an additional perspective. It imposes limits not only on the state but also on parents. It insists that children's best interests must be a primary consideration in all matters affecting them, that their views must be given serious consideration and that the child's evolving capacities must be respected. In other words, the Convention affects the right of parents to freedom of choice in their child's education; parental rights to choose their children's education are not absolute and are seen to decline as children grow older. The rationale behind parental choice is not to legitimize a denial of their child's rights. Rather, it is to prevent any state monopoly of education and to protect educational pluralism. In the case of conflict between a parental choice and the best interests of the child, however, the child should always be the priority.

The right to education thus involves these three principal players: the state, the parent and the child. There is a triangular relationship between them, and in the development of rights-based education it is important to bear in mind that their differing objectives need to be reconciled. In addition, other actors with a significant contribution and responsibility include teachers, the local community, policymakers, the media and the private sector.

## Balancing rights and responsibilities of children

Human rights are not contingent on the exercise of responsibility. They are innate and universal. There is no requirement on the part of a child, for example, that she or he demonstrate a responsible attitude in order to 'earn' an entitlement to education. Nevertheless, there is a direct and complex relationship between rights and responsibilities, rooted in the reciprocal and mutual nature of human rights.

All children have a right to learn. This means they are entitled to an effective learning environment in multiple spaces, not just the school setting and at the primary level. It also implies that they have responsibilities to ensure their behaviour does not deny that right to other children. All children are entitled to express their views and have them given due weight. This involves listening as well as talking. It requires that children play a part in the creation of constructive spaces that promote mutual respect. And as teachers have responsibilities for children's rights, so children, too, have responsibilities towards teachers. The same principles of mutual respect apply between children and adults. The right to protection from violence extends to both children and adults, and places a responsibility on children to avoid the use of aggression or physical violence. While teachers bear responsibility for preparing lessons, teaching, grading work, maintaining positive classroom discipline and creating opportunities for children to express views, so children carry responsibilities for undertaking their work, collaborating with other children, keeping the classroom in order and, so far as it is within their means, arriving regularly and on time.

One of the most effective means of promoting children's understanding of the reciprocal basis of rights is to create an environment where their own rights are respected. Through this experience, they develop the capacities to exercise responsibility.

## Tensions in the implementation of a rights-based approach

In a rights-based approach to education, founded on principles of universality and equity, there are inevitable tensions that arise in the process of implementation. Some of these are associated with limits on resources and can only be addressed through a commitment to progressive realization. Some derive from insufficient understanding of the concept of rights or the potential strategies that can be adopted to resolve them. The rest of this chapter considers a number of these tensions. There are no straightforward solutions to many of them, but Chapters 3 and 4 provide some indications of approaches that can be taken to reconcile them, consistent with a commitment to the human rights of all.

## Access and quality

Where resources are scarce, the requirement to make education universally available can mean a reduction in the per capita funding for each child – leading to higher teacher-student ratios, overcrowded classes, fewer materials and resources per class, and lower building standards – thereby sacrificing quality for access. In these circumstances, access to education is an overriding concern, and it is not acceptable to discriminate between groups of children and offer preferential treatment to some on the basis of resources. Yet, whenever possible, efforts need to be made to increase the budgetary allocation to ensure there is access to quality education for all children. A tendency to discriminate must be guarded against, and donors may need to ensure that funding is dedicated to the provision of education without discrimination on any grounds.

## Equity and efficiency

The approaches necessary to make schooling available for all children may be less efficient and cost-effective. Although it may be more expensive to develop small satellite schools in villages, for example, this may be the only way of encouraging parents to allow young girls to attend. It may be more economically efficient to place all children who do not speak the national language in a separate school, but doing so may deny them the right to an education on an equal basis with other children. It is important to consult with children, parents and communities to explore what will work most effectively in their environment. This will help build a sense of ownership and collaboration in finding solutions that will best strengthen access to education. There is little point in designing a cost-effective system that is rejected by the local community.

## Universality and diversity

The respect for difference and the right to be different in regard to cultural, linguistic and religious identity needs to be reconciled with the universal right to education as part of a broader set of human rights. Approaches to education provision that ensure universal education for all need to be undertaken with due regard for local and regional differences, particularly in regard to language and culture. Failure to do so implies a failure to reach out to all communities.

## Priorities and trade-offs

Scarce resources can lead to trade-offs, such as the decision to invest in primary education at the cost of limiting access to secondary education, or to postpone the development of educational opportunities for children with disabilities. Realistically, it is not possible for all governments to fulfil their obligations to ensure the right to education for all children immediately. However, where financial and human resources are limited, the principle of progressive realization requires governments to have a clear strategy and time frame for achieving the objective of universal access to primary and secondary education, and each action should be conducive to the full realization of the right to education for all.

## Outcomes and process

Pressure to achieve such targets as the Millennium Development Goals may lead to strategies that are designed to produce immediate results but fail to invest in long-term social change to sustain a genuine commitment to and capacity for meaningful education. For example, an increased number of school places and teachers may lead to higher levels of enrolment, only to result in increased drop-out rates because no accommodation has been made to children's particular circumstances. Ensuring attendance, completion and reasonable attainment in school involves consultations with children and parents; policies to address poverty; the development of more relevant curricula; and respect for children's rights in school, including the abolition of physical and humiliating punishments.

## Emergency responses in the short and longer term

In emergencies, the immediate focus is inevitably on survival and the provision of food, water, shelter and medical treatment. For children, however, the immediate re-introduction of education is not only a right but can also be a vital resource in restoring normality, overcoming psychosocial trauma, building capacities for survival and providing structure out of chaos. There are a growing number of positive examples of programmes designed to provide immediate schooling in the aftermath of crises (see 'Situations of risk' on page 61). Ensuring that a maximum number of children attend school under these difficult circumstances has to be balanced, however, with the parallel need to guarantee quality education in the short and longer term.

## Teachers' and children's rights

It is sometimes argued by teachers that affording respect for the rights of children diminishes respect for their own rights. They may erroneously believe that prohibiting physical punishment or involving students in decisions diminishes their position or makes it more difficult to maintain discipline. This view derives from an assumption that rights represent a fixed quantity of entitlement and that giving more to one constituency necessarily deprives the other. It also derives from an authoritarian understanding of the teacher-child relationship. While respecting the rights of children does involve some transfer of power, this does not necessitate the loss of rights on the part of the teacher. In practice, without mutual respect, the pedagogic relationship is fragile. Creating a school environment in which children's rights are respected is more likely to enhance respect for the role of the teacher, although this outcome can only be achieved if teachers are appropriately supported and resourced.

## Work and school

Controversy about the role of work in children's lives continues.[20] There are tensions associated with the extent to which it, on the one hand, provides preparation for life, and on the other, impedes educational outcomes. There is no consensus as to whether there are forms of work that are acceptable and can be accommodated alongside the right to education – or whether all child work should be prohibited during the years of compulsory schooling. The Convention on the Rights of the Child makes clear that children must be protected from all forms of work that are harmful to their development or that interfere with their education. International Labour Organization (ILO) Convention 182 elaborates the worst forms of child labour and makes clear governments' obligations to protect all children from these areas of work. Governments need to introduce legislation and policies that guarantee these protections. It is also incumbent on governments to provide education that offers a viable alternative to employment in terms of its quality and relevance; to introduce policies that address the poverty and livelihood insecurity that force many children into work; and to make education sufficiently flexible and inclusive to allow those children to attend who have no choice but to work.

# A RIGHTS-BASED CONCEPTUAL FRAMEWORK FOR EDUCATION

## INTRODUCTION

The development of a human rights-based approach to education requires a framework that addresses the right of access to education, the right to quality education and respect for human rights in education. These dimensions are interdependent and interlinked, and a rights-based education necessitates the realization of all three.

The right to education requires a commitment to ensuring universal access, including taking all necessary measures to reach the most marginalized children. But getting children into schools is not enough; it is no guarantee of an education that enables individuals to achieve their economic and social objectives and to acquire the skills, knowledge, values and attitudes that bring about responsible and active citizenship. A study by the Southern and Eastern African Consortium for Monitoring Educational Quality (1995–1998), for example, measures primary school students' reading literacy against standards established by national reading experts and sixth-grade teachers. In four out of seven countries, fewer than half of sixth grade students achieved minimum competence in reading.[21] Poor achievement is also evident in a study conducted by the *Programme d'Analyse des Systèmes Éducatifs de la CONFEMEN* (PASEC) in six French-speaking African countries in 1996–2001: Achievement levels were "low" in French or mathematics for up to 43 per cent of fifth grade pupils in all six countries, and more than 40 per cent of students in Senegal struggled to put several numbers with two decimal points in order.[22] Achieving a quality education is also a challenge in industrialized nations. Recent studies show that large numbers of students in rich countries do not acquire the basic skills to be competent in today's world.[23]

To ensure quality education in line with the Dakar Framework for Action (2002) and the aims of education elaborated by the Committee on the Rights of the Child,[24] attention must be paid to the relevance of the curriculum, the role of teachers, and the nature and ethos of the learning environment. A rights-based approach necessitates a commitment to recognizing and respecting the human rights of children while they are in school – including respect for their identity, agency and integrity. This will contribute to increased retention rates and also makes the process of education empowering, participatory, transparent and accountable. In addition, children will continue to be excluded from education unless measures are taken to address their rights to freedom from discrimination, to an adequate standard of living and to meaningful participation. A quality education cannot be achieved without regard to children's right to health and well-being. Children cannot achieve their optimum development when they are subjected to humiliating punishment or physical abuse.

This conceptual framework highlights the need for a holistic approach to education, reflecting the universality and indivisibility of all human rights. The following sections set out the central elements that therefore need to be addressed in each of the three dimensions mentioned above.

| | | |
|---|---|---|
| **1.** | **The right of access to education** | • Education throughout all stages of childhood and beyond |
| | | • Availability and accessibility of education |
| | | • Equality of opportunity |
| **2.** | **The right to quality education** | • A broad, relevant and inclusive curriculum |
| | | • Rights-based learning and assessment |
| | | • Child-friendly, safe and healthy environments |
| **3.** | **The right to respect in the learning environment** | • Respect for identity |
| | | • Respect for participation rights |
| | | • Respect for integrity |

# 1.  THE RIGHT OF ACCESS TO EDUCATION

## Obligations to ensure the right of access to education

- Provide free and compulsory primary education.

- Develop forms of secondary education that are available and accessible to everyone, and introduce measures to provide free education and financial assistance in cases of need.

- Provide higher education that is accessible on the basis of capacity by every appropriate means.

- Provide accessible educational and vocational information and guidance.

- Introduce measures to encourage regular attendance and reduce drop-out rates.

- Provide education on the basis of equal opportunity.

- Ensure respect for the right to education without discrimination of any kind on any grounds.

- Ensure an inclusive education system at all levels.

- Provide reasonable accommodation and support measures to ensure that children with disabilities have effective access to and receive education in a manner conducive to achieving the fullest possible social integration.

- Ensure an adequate standard of living for physical, mental, spiritual, moral and social development.

- Provide protection and assistance to ensure respect for the rights of children who are refugees or seeking asylum.

- Provide protection from economic exploitation and work that interferes with education.

**Sources:** Article 26, Universal Declaration of Human Rights; articles 2, 22, 23, 27, 28 and 32, Convention on the Rights of the Child; article 13, International Covenant on Economic, Social and Cultural Rights; article 10, Convention on the Elimination of All Forms of Discrimination against Women; articles 4 and 5, UNESCO Convention against Discrimination in Education; article 24, Convention on the Rights of Persons with Disabilities (opened for signature 30 March 2007).

The right of access to education comprises three elements: the provision of education throughout all stages of childhood and beyond, consistent with the Education for All goals; the provision of sufficient, accessible school places or learning opportunities; and equality of opportunity.

## Education throughout all stages of childhood and beyond

Learning is a lifelong process. A rights-based approach to education seeks to build opportunities for children to achieve their optimum capacities throughout their childhood and beyond. It requires a life-cycle approach, investing in learning and ensuring effective transitions at each stage of the child's life.

Although the Convention on the Rights of the Child does not impose explicit obligations to provide early childhood education, the Committee on the Rights of the Child interprets the right to education as beginning at birth and as closely linked to the child's right to maximum development. It calls on governments to ensure that young children have access to programmes of health care and education designed to promote their well-being, and stresses that the right to optimum development implies the right to education during early childhood, with systematic and quality family involvement.

Quality education during the early years plays a vital part in promoting readiness for school and is also the best guarantee of promoting sustainable economic and social development, and attaining the Millennium Development Goals and the Education for All and A World Fit for Children goals.[25] A study of children in Nepal shows that more than 95 per cent of children who had attended a non-formal preschool facility enrolled in primary school, where they also performed better than those who had not attended. Around 80 per cent of the first group passed grade one, compared to around 60 per cent of the group without preschool experience.[26]

While human rights law affirms that every child is entitled to free, compulsory primary education, obligations in respect of secondary education are less emphatic. The duty is to encourage its development and make it available and accessible to every child, and free where possible. The weaker formulation does not reflect a lesser commitment to secondary education, but rather a recognition that it is currently beyond the resources of many countries to make it free and compulsory.[27] Since these conventions were drafted, there has been an increasing recognition of the fundamental importance of secondary education.

Moreover, development does not cease at age 18. Education can and should take place throughout life consistent with the third goal of Education for All, which calls for meeting the learning needs of all young people and adults through access to learning and life skills programmes. Governments should support the achievement of a strong base for lifelong learning, through education directed towards responsible autonomy, self-directed learning and preparation for full citizenship.

## Availability and accessibility of education

States have obligations to establish the legislative and policy framework, together with sufficient resources, to fulfil the right to education for every child. Each child must therefore be provided with an available school place or learning opportunity, together with appropriately qualified teachers and adequate and appropriate resources and equipment.[28] The level of provision of primary education must be consistent with the numbers of children entitled to receive it.

All learning environments must be both physically and economically accessible for every child, including the most marginalized. It is important to recognize that a school that is accessible to one child may not be accessible to another. Schools must be within safe physical reach or accessible through technology (for example, access to a 'distance learning' programme). They must also be affordable to all.[29]

## Equality of opportunity

Every child has an equal right to attend school. Making schools accessible and available is an important first step in fulfilling this right but not sufficient to ensure its realization.[30] Equality of opportunity can only be achieved by removing barriers in the community and in schools.

Even where schools exist, economic, social and cultural factors – including gender, disability, AIDS, household poverty, ethnicity, minority status, orphanhood and child labour – often interlink to keep children out of school. Governments have obligations to develop legislation, policies and support services to remove barriers in the family and community that impede children's access to school.

Schools can directly or indirectly impede the access of some children, for example, through reflecting a male-dominated culture, pervading patterns of violence and sexual abuse or prevailing societal norms, such as caste bias. Negative teacher attitudes towards girls, biases in the curriculum, lack of female teachers and role models, and lack of adequate access to hygiene and sanitation can also inhibit enrolment and contribute to poor attainment and high drop-out levels.[31] Schools may refuse to accept children with disabilities or AIDS. Inflexibility in school systems may exclude many working children. Governments should take action to ensure the provision of education that is both inclusive and non-discriminatory and that is adapted to ensure the equal opportunity of every child to attend.

# 2. THE RIGHT TO QUALITY EDUCATION

## Obligations to ensure the right to quality education

- Develop children's personalities, talents, and mental and physical abilities to their fullest potential.

- Promote respect for human rights and fundamental freedoms, and prepare children for a responsible life in a spirit of peace, tolerance, equality and friendship.

- Promote respect for the child's, his or her parents' and others' cultural identity, language and values.

- Promote respect for the natural environment.

- Ensure the child's access to information from a diversity of sources.

- Ensure that the best interests of children are a primary consideration.

- Promote respect for the evolving capacities of children in the exercise of their rights.

- Respect the right of children to rest, leisure, play, recreation, and participation in arts and culture.

**Sources:** Article 26, Universal Declaration of Human Rights; articles 3, 5, 6, 12, 17, 29, 31, Convention on the Rights of the Child; article 13, International Covenant on Economic, Social and Cultural Rights; and article 24, International Convention on the Rights of Persons with Disabilities (opened for signature 30 March 2007).

The Dakar Framework for Action commits nations to the provision of primary education of good quality and to improving all aspects of educational quality.[32] Although there is no single definition of 'quality', most attempts to define it incorporate two fundamental perspectives. First, cognitive development is a primary objective of education, with the effectiveness of education measured against its success in achieving this objective. Second, education must promote creative and emotional development, supporting the objectives of peace, citizenship and security, fostering equality and passing global and local cultural values down to future generations.

These perspectives have been integrated into the aims of education set out in the Convention on the Rights of the Child, which formulates a philosophy of respect for children as individuals, recognizing each child as "unique – in characteristics, interests, abilities and needs."[33] It sets out a framework of obligations to provide education that promotes children's optimum development. Article 29 implies "the need for education to be child-centred, child-friendly and empowering, and it highlights the need for educational processes to be based on the very principles it enunciates."[34] Every child has a right to an education that empowers him or her by developing life skills, learning and other capacities, self-esteem and self-confidence. The provision of a quality education demands attention to the content of the curriculum, the nature of the teaching and the quality of the learning environment. It implies a need for the creation of flexible, effective and respectful learning environments that are responsive to the needs of all children.

## A broad, relevant and inclusive curriculum

Common guidance is provided in all the key human rights treaties for the development of the curriculum, indicating an underlying global consensus on the content and scope necessary for a rights-based education.

The curriculum must enable every child to acquire the core academic curriculum and basic cognitive skills, together with essential life skills that equip children to face life challenges, make well-balanced decisions and develop a healthy lifestyle, good social relationships, critical thinking and the capacity for non-violent conflict resolution. It must develop respect for human rights and fundamental freedoms, and promote respect for different cultures and values and for the natural environment. The Committee on the Rights of the Child stipulates that the curriculum, both in early childhood provision and in school, "must be of direct relevance to the child's social, cultural, environmental and economic context, and to his or her present and future needs and take full account of the child's evolving capacities"[35] (*see Appendix V, page 128*).

The curriculum must be inclusive and tailored to the needs of children in different or difficult circumstances. All teaching and learning materials should be free from gender stereotypes and from harmful or negative representations of any ethnic or indigenous groups. To enable all children with disabilities to fulfil their potential, provision must be made to enable them to, for example, learn Braille, orientation or sign language.

## Rights-based learning and assessment

The way in which children are provided with the opportunity to learn is as important as what they learn. Traditional models of schooling that silence children and perceive them as passive recipients are not consistent with a rights-based approach to learning.

There should be respect for the agency of children and young people, who should be recognized as active contributors to their own learning, rather than passive recipients of education.[36] There should also be respect for the evolving and differing capacities of children, together with recognition that children do not acquire skills and knowledge at fixed or predetermined ages.[37] Teaching and learning must involve a variety of interactive methodologies to create stimulating and participatory environments. Rather than simply transmitting knowledge, educators involved in creating or strengthening learning opportunities should facilitate participatory learning. Learning environments should be child friendly and conducive to the optimum development of children's capacities.

Assessment of learning achievement is vital. Testing enables schools to identify learning needs and develop targeted initiatives to provide support to individual children. Analysis of results enables governments to assess whether they are achieving their educational objectives and to adjust policy and resources accordingly. Dissemination of results is a necessary aspect of accountability and transparency in education and facilitates discussions on the quality of education. At the same time, a commitment to realizing children's rights to their optimum capacities implies the need for sensitive and constructive methods of appraising and monitoring children's' work that take account of their differing abilities and do not discriminate against those with particular learning needs.

## A child-friendly, safe and healthy environment

The obligation to give primacy to the best interests of children and to ensure their optimum development requires that learning environments are welcoming, gender sensitive, healthy, safe and protective. Although situations of extreme poverty, emergency and conflict may often impede this, children should never be expected to attend schools where the environment is detrimental to their health and well-being. Schools should take measures to contribute towards children's health and well-being, taking into account the differing needs of children. This will necessitate measures to ensure that obstacles to health and safety are removed – for example, consideration as to the location of schools, travel to and from school, factors that might cause illness or accidents in the classroom or playgrounds, and appropriate facilities for girls. It also requires the proactive provision of facilities, services and policies to promote the health and safety of children and the active participation of the local community. A healthy environment also needs to provide safe and stimulating opportunities for play and recreation.

## 3. THE RIGHT TO RESPECT IN THE LEARNING ENVIRONMENT

### Obligations to respect children's rights in the learning environment

- Respect every child equally without discrimination on any grounds.

- Teach respect for human rights and fundamental freedoms, for difference and for life in a society where there is understanding, peace, tolerance, equality and friendship.

- Give primary consideration to the best interests of the child.

- Respect the evolving capacities of the child.

- Respect the right of children to express their views on all matters of concern to them and have those views given due weight in accordance with children's age and maturity.

- Recognize the right to freedom of expression, religion, conscience, thought and assembly.

- Respect the privacy of children.

- Take all appropriate measures to ensure that school discipline is administered in a manner consistent with the child's dignity and all other rights in the Convention on the Rights of the Child.

- Protect children from all forms of physical violence, injury or abuse, neglect or negligence, maltreatment or exploitation, including sexual abuse.

**Sources:** Articles 2, 3, 5, 12, 13, 14, 15, 16, 19, 28, 29, Convention on the Rights of the Child; articles 1, 2, Universal Declaration of Human Rights; articles 18, 19, 27, International Covenant of Civil and Political Rights.

Human rights are inalienable. In other words, they are inherent in each human being. Accordingly, they must be respected in all learning environments. The right to education must be understood as incorporating respect for children's identity, their right to express their views on all matters of concern to them, and their physical and personal integrity.

### Respect for identity

UNESCO's Convention against Discrimination in Education (1960) protects the educational rights of national minorities. Depending on the educational policy of each State, it establishes the right to use or be taught in one's own language, provided this does not exclude minorities from understanding the language and culture of the community as a whole and that it is not provided at a lower standard than the one generally provided. The Convention on the Protection and Promotion of Diversity in Cultural Expressions (2005) introduces obligations to respect cultural diversity, including through educational programmes.

In addition, article 30 of the Convention on the Rights of the Child stresses the right of children to enjoy their own culture, practice their own religion and use their own language. International human rights law also requires States to respect the freedom of parents to decide the kind of education they would like for their child. Governments are entitled to determine which religion, if any, should be taught in schools, as well as the medium of instruction for schools. And finally, the Convention on the Rights of the Child, in its recognition of the right of children to express their views on all matters of concern to them and to have those views given due weight, introduces a further dimension to the issue of choice and freedom in education provision. Thus, it is in the arena of these cultural rights that the tensions discussed in Chapter 1 between children, parents and governments in respect of education are often most sharply drawn.

There is no simple solution to these tensions, nor any one correct approach. Whatever approach is adopted, however, governments have obligations to ensure that children do not experience discrimination, that respect is afforded to their culture and religion, and that every effort is made to prevent social exclusion and educational disadvantage as a consequence of speaking a minority language. In determining the most appropriate system for addressing respect for identity, a rights-based approach requires that children, families and communities are consulted and involved. And if relevant obligations are not being fulfilled, mechanisms should be in place to challenge schools, education authorities and the government.

## Respect for participation rights

Article 12 of the Convention on the Rights of the Child establishes that children are entitled to express their views on all matters of concern to them and to have these given due weight in accordance with their age and maturity. This principle of participation is affirmed by other rights to freedom of expression, religion and association. These rights apply to all aspects of their education and have profound implications for the status of children throughout the education system. Participation rights do not simply extend to the pedagogic relationships in the classroom but also across the school and in the development of legislation and policy. The Committee on the Rights of the Child has frequently recommended that governments take steps to encourage greater participation by children in schools.[38] Children can also play an important role in advocating for the realization of their rights. Governments need to introduce legislation and policy to establish and support these rights at all levels in the education system (*see Appendix VI, page 131*).

## Respect for integrity

The Convention demands not only that children are protected from all forms of violence but also that school discipline is administered in a manner consistent with the child's dignity. However, frequent and severe violence, including emotional abuse and humiliation in school, remains widespread in countries throughout the world.[39] The Committee on the Rights of the Child has consistently argued that such punishments constitute a violation of the rights of the child and a denial of children's integrity. Much violence is also perpetrated by children against children and children against teachers, and it is equally important to challenge such behaviour.

Physical and other forms of humiliating and abusive treatment are not only a violation of the child's right to protection from violence, but also highly counterproductive to learning. Children cite violence as a significant factor contributing to school dropout.[40] Furthermore, it diminishes self-esteem and promotes the message that violence is acceptable. Many factors contribute to the continued use of violence towards children in schools, including:

- Social and legal acceptance of violence against children.
- Lack of adequate training for teachers, resulting in poor classroom management and a consequent breakdown of discipline.
- Lack of knowledge of the benefits associated with positive discipline and how to promote it.
- A failure to understand the harmful impact of physical punishment.
- Lack of understanding of the different ways in which children learn, and the fact that children will differ in their development and their capacities to understand.

Action must be taken to address all these barriers and to achieve rights-respecting educational environments in which all forms of physical and humiliating punishments are prohibited and a commitment to non-violent conflict resolution is promoted.

© UNESCO/30204607 063/Gert Van Dermeersch

# STATE OBLIGATIONS AND GOVERNMENT RESPONSIBILITIES

Once States ratify international human rights instruments, they commit themselves, through whichever government is in power, to compliance with the rights embodied in those instruments. States hold the primary responsibilities and are accountable to the holders of those rights for their implementation.

To ensure the realization of the right to education for all children, States have three levels of obligations:

- **To fulfil the right to education** by ensuring that education is available for all children and that positive measures are taken to enable children to benefit from it, for example, by tackling poverty, adapting the curricula to the needs of all children or engaging parents to enable them to provide effective support to their children's education.
- **To respect the right to education** by avoiding any action that would serve to prevent children accessing education, for example, legislation that categorizes certain groups of children with disabilities as uneducable.
- **To protect the right to education** by taking the necessary measures to remove the barriers to education posed by individuals or communities, for example, cultural barriers to education or violence and abuse in the school environment.[41]

This chapter focuses on the political and economic environment, the legislative framework and the education policies that are needed to fulfil these three obligations in relation to the right of access to education, to quality education and to respect for human rights in education. Underlying all three is the need to have regard to the best interests of every child.[42]

# CREATING A SUPPORTIVE POLITICAL AND ECONOMIC ENVIRONMENT

Education does not exist in a vacuum. Ensuring that every child has access to quality and respectful learning environments throughout his or her childhood necessitates action far beyond ministries of education. The right to education can only be realized in a political and economic environment that acknowledges the importance of transparent, participatory and accountable processes, as well as broad-based collaboration both across government and in the wider society. It needs a long-term strategic commitment to the provision of adequate resources, development of cross-departmental structures, engagement with the energies and capacities of parents and local communities, and partnership with non-governmental organizations.

## Progressive realization of education rights

Both the Convention on the Rights of the Child (article 4) and the International Covenant on Economic, Social and Cultural Rights (articles 2 and 13) require that States undertake all appropriate legislative, administrative and other measures to the maximum extent of their available resources for the implementation of education rights. There will always be fiscal constraints, but it is possible to manoeuvre to better allocate resources. Countries with very similar gross domestic products can and do apportion very different levels of investment in education. The committees that monitor these treaties have both argued that "even where the available resources are demonstrably inadequate, the obligation remains for a State party to strive to ensure the widest possible enjoyment of relevant rights under prevailing circumstances."[43]

Governments need to develop strategic plans for the progressive realization of educational rights that include a time frame for the introduction of measures to extend access to both primary and secondary education, raise the quality of education and introduce the necessary legislative and policy measures to ensure the protection of children's rights in schools. If States fail to meet minimum core obligations, such as universal access to free, compulsory primary education, they are required to demonstrate that every effort has been made to use all resources available to satisfy as a matter of priority those minimum obligations.[44]

## A conducive political environment

### Political will and commitment

One of the most important prerequisites in realizing rights, especially those related to such global public goods as education, health or water and sanitation, is the presence of firm in-country political will and commitment. In many countries around the world, good policy formulations exist on paper but are not translated into action. Real decisions at the stage of implementation are taken at the time of preparation of action plans and projects or during budget allocations. States need to demonstrate the political will to follow up and implement such policy commitments on the ground.

### Capacity-building and development

As a rights-based approach to education places the primary responsibility for ensuring good quality education on the state, consideration needs to be given to whether it has the capacity – in terms of managerial, human and financial resources – to analyse, organize and provide all the inputs necessary to make meaningful education a reality for those who are left out of the system. Many government programmes worldwide have tried to reach out to marginalized groups of children but have lacked the capacity to work simultaneously on several fronts – access, quality and respect. Thus, the role of capacity-building and development becomes crucial. While some States – for example, those in transition or just emerging out of conflict – require capacity-building such as teacher training or curriculum development, others may require capacity development in terms of working with the state bureaucracy to train their officials to reform legal and regulatory frameworks, as well as the systems for implementing them.

### Good governance

Factors relating to good governance – such as demanding accountability, ensuring transparency, access to justice and the rule of law, and enlisting stakeholder participation, through, for instance, devolution policies or in budgetary analysis – are essential 'on the ground' enabling conditions.

## Mechanisms for claiming rights and holding governments accountable

Access to the courts can be an effective means of challenging the failure of the State to, for example, make adequate provision for education, achieve equality of opportunity or protect children whose rights are violated in the education system. A successful illustration of the use of legal redress is provided by a small disability organization in Nepal that took the Government to the Supreme Court to argue that the failure to provide additional time in public examinations for blind children denied them the right to equality of opportunity in education, given that Braille takes longer to read and write. The Court decreed that blind children should be entitled to extra time in examinations to reflect this difference.

Legal mechanisms are not the only means of achieving accountability. Others include:

- Transparency – ensuring that people understand how and what decisions are being made, what resources are being provided to support the right to education and establishing public processes for regular reporting on progress.

- Information – rights are meaningless unless people are aware that they exist and that governments have obligations with regard to their implementation.

- Participation – creating effective consultative processes that offer meaningful opportunities for marginalized groups, including children, to contribute their experience and expertise to the development of education policy and provision.

- Parliamentary accountability – establishing all-party parliamentary committees to scrutinize government action and hold it accountable for its obligations to respect the right to education.

**Source:** (for Nepal example): Lansdown, Gerison, *Disabled Children in Nepal: Progress in implementing the Convention on the Rights of the Child*, Rights for Disabled Children/Disability Awareness in Action, London, 2003, <www.daa.org.uk/RDC%20Nepal.htm>, accessed 10 July 2007.

### Devolution of authority

In many countries, policies and budgets are still managed at the national level, reducing the potential for the delivery of education to address the local needs of communities and for community-based involvement and ownership of children's education. Consideration should be given to the need to balance, on the one hand, the establishment of a national framework consistent with the universal human right to education with, on the other, the potential value of devolution of the day-to-day implementation and management of the budgets for delivering the education service to district or community levels.

Devolved authority, if accompanied by greater accountability and transparency, can serve to address corruption, empower local communities and utilize local expertise and knowledge. There should always be systems in place to ensure that communities and other stakeholders can participate in the management of the local education system and create or expand other complementary learning opportunities. Devolution must also be accompanied by a clear and sustainable effort to provide the necessary technical and financial support to guarantee the quality of education desired. Devolved authority without the resources to implement it is no solution.

## Improving outcomes through devolution of authority to schools

Devolving authority to the school level is a form of educational reform that has been gaining support in developing countries. School-based management programmes are now being implemented in countries and areas including the Hong Kong Special Administrative Region of China, El Salvador, Indonesia, Kenya, Kyrgyzstan, Mexico, Nepal, Nicaragua and Paraguay. They involve a shift in responsibility and decision-making to principals, teachers, parents and students. In Mexico, for example, the programme began in 1996 with monetary support and training. By 2005, more than 45 per cent of primary schools had implemented school-based management. These schools were located in disadvantaged areas where educational outcomes were below average. Research indicates these programmes have been an effective measure in improving outcomes and reducing grade failure and repetition.

Source: Gertler, Paul, Harry Patrinos and Marta Rubio-Codina, 'Empowering Parents to Improve Education: Evidence from rural Mexico', Policy Research Working Paper 3935, World Bank, Washington, D.C., 2006, p. 2.

## Rights-based analysis and planning

### Sector-wide approaches

Sector-wide approaches (SWAps) to education, which are evolving in the new aid environment, provide a possible framework in which a rights-based approach to education can be achieved. They involve the development of a government-led single education strategy that is then supported by all externally funded initiatives. In other words, they ensure an integrated and coherent policy rather than a series of separately funded and possibly contradictory projects with different objectives and time frames. They have been found to be an effective framework through which to strengthen education policy, particularly in eastern and southern Africa.[45]

However, it is imperative that both governments and international donors ensure that human rights are fully integrated into sector-wide approaches and provide the core principles on which they are developed.[46] In particular, the four underlying principles of the Convention on the Rights of the Child – namely, non-discrimination, the best interests of the child, the optimum development of the child, and the right to express views and have them given due weight – need to inform the education strategy. Sector-wide approaches should incorporate measures to address all three dimensions of a rights-based approach to education – access, quality and respect for rights – through an inclusive approach addressing the needs of all children. Without this breadth, the wider barriers that impede the right to education will not be tackled. For example, a study undertaken in 2002 found that many existing sector-wide approaches focus on a narrow investment in girls' education, rather than addressing the underlying issues that lead to inequality of access.[47] Education strategies and plans need to take into account the relevant recommendations made by the UN Committees on the Rights of the Child and on the Elimination of Discrimination against Women. These measures will serve to strengthen a commitment to child-centred education. They also need to take account of the views and experiences of stakeholders at the community level, including children.

**Macroeconomic policy**

Macroeconomic policy should reflect the commitment to the right to education, including the allocation of an appropriate level of resources. Actual budget levels are arbitrary, but the Education for All Fast Track Initiative – a partnership among donors and multilateral agencies, set up in 2002 to support low-income countries in funding sound education plans and managed by the World Bank – provides a framework for guiding education initiatives. According to benchmarks it established, public domestically generated government revenues for education as a percentage of the gross domestic product should be between 14 and 18 per cent; education spending as a share of government revenues should be 20 per cent; and primary education spending as a share of total education expenditure should be between 42 and 64 per cent, depending on the length of the cycle.[48]

## A human rights-based approach to budgetary analysis

A rights-based approach to budgetary analysis in respect of education will require consideration of the following principles:

- The obligation to undertake all measures to the maximum extent of available resources to implement the right to education. Progressive realization of the right to education means a specific and continuing obligation to move as expeditiously and effectively as possible towards implementation of this right.

- The obligation to ensure that the best interests of children are a primary consideration. The Committee on the Rights of the Child has emphasized that this requires that children are prioritized in resource allocation, in particular in respect of the right to free primary education for all.

- Non-discrimination in the allocation of funding – for example, equitable amounts for rural schools or children from particular ethnic groups.

- The obligation to take deliberate, concrete and targeted steps towards the full realization of the right to education.

The process for budgetary analysis will need to address:

- Situation analyses and costing studies based on an assessment of the attainment outcomes that are expected, together with the level of resources that will be necessary to achieve those outcomes.

- Cost analyses that take account of the differing needs of children, including children with disabilities.*

- Distribution of budgets for different levels of education and provision of funding for national and local services.

- Opportunities for participation and consultation by rights holders, including children themselves.

- Transparency in order to promote monitoring and accountability. Budgets are a useful instrument through which to assess and make visible how well the State is responding to the duty to implement education rights.

**Sources:** Committee on Economic, Social and Cultural Rights, 'General Comment No. 13: The right to education (article 13)', E/C.12/1999/10, December 1999. (* Lawrence, John, *The Right to Education for Persons with Disabilities: Towards inclusion – An EFA flagship paper*, Inclusion International, London, 2004, p. 17.)

**Wider economic policy**

The wider economic policy can also have a direct or indirect impact on the rights-based approach to education. The Committee on the Rights of the Child has argued that States must be guided by the 'best interests' principle in respect of budgetary priorities in the allocation of available resources.[49] Yet, too often, the impact of economic policies on children is given no consideration, despite the fact that no economic policy is child-neutral.[50] Policies that appear to have very little impact on children will often, in practice, have a bias for or against their interests. For example, policies relating to trade barriers, economic growth and taxation can have implications on children's overall well-being, their parents' capacities to support access to education and the quality of education provided. National Plans of Action, including poverty reduction strategy papers, need to reflect the commitment to the right to education.

## Disaggregated data collection, monitoring and evaluation

**Measurement of outcomes**

A rights-based approach to education is characterized by accountability and transparency, and thus its outcomes must be measurable. Students need to know how well they are doing, how they can improve and what they can aspire to. Families and communities want to know if the school is providing children with skills that will be beneficial to the children themselves, as well as the community, especially if there are competing demands on children's time and high costs associated with education. They also need to know about the readiness of the school to receive their children and give them a good start in lifelong learning. Teachers need to know what children are learning, what works and how to measure that learning. Schools need to know if teachers are doing an effective job. Education departments want to know if student learning is consistent with curriculum standards, if schooling is efficient and if students are well prepared for the challenges of life. Governments need data to plan and ensure availability of quality education for all. International agencies want data that is comparable in order to assess global progress in attainment of positive learning outcomes.[51] Mechanisms therefore need to be introduced to measure and monitor access, quality and respect for rights in education, in terms of both individual children and the education system as a whole.

## School report cards: Promoting accountability and transparency

A number of countries are experimenting with information systems at the school level known as 'school report cards'. Some of these systems measure school performance, while others provide school managers with participatory diagnostic and management tools. The aims vary from an increase in accountability and transparency to community mobilization or improved school management. There are also a number of different formats, but the report cards fall broadly into four categories. At the basic level, the cards include information on the number of students, teachers, textbooks and classrooms and on expenditure. At the next level, they include measures of efficiency including repetition and drop-out rates, parental and community involvement, and school safety. The third level incorporates data on educational outputs, graduation rates and text scores, and the final level also addresses student and parental satisfaction with the school.

There is some evidence that school report cards are effective in achieving their objectives. However, there are also concerns about their sustainability. Factors that inform sustainability include the ability of the audience to use them effectively, the capacity of available systems to produce accurate and timely information and the existence of political will at a senior political level and at the level of the principal or director of the schools.

**Source:** United States Agency for International Development, 'School Report Cards: Some Recent Experiences', *Equip2 Working Paper*, USAID, Washington DC, 2006.

## Data collection

Accurate data are needed on the preschool and school-aged population so that appropriate education provision can be made for every child. Emphasis should be placed on data that are not only quantitative and disaggregated but also qualitative. Such qualitative data can help in measuring the degree of enjoyment of human rights in a particular sector – for example, the improvement of quality of learning in schools via the types of teaching aids used, or the level of interaction of the teachers. Capturing of qualitative data is far more effective if it is undertaken in partnership with local communities, which have knowledge of the social, cultural and economic factors that need to inform the location, design and target populations of schools *(see also 'Communities' on page 90)*. It is thus necessary, at the local level, to build accurate information about local communities to inform decisions about educational provision and plan for the right of access to education for all children.

In addition, disaggregated data are needed on the patterns of enrolment, attendance, completion and attainment of children in the education system, including by gender, disability, geography, ethnicity, class and religion. Data also need to encompass the numbers of children enrolled in private schools, including faith-based schools. Generic data can too easily disguise hidden pockets of inequality and render discriminatory patterns of access invisible. Disaggregated data will provide information to guide policy in respect of, for example, numbers and location of schools, potential review of the curriculum, teacher training, targeted measures to tackle child labour, bilingual teaching and gender discrimination.

To date, the data collected on children's education are usually limited to enrolment, attendance and formal attainment. There are few indicators developed to monitor the broader dimensions of a rights-based approach to education. New indicators that capture both the quantitative and qualitative aspects are needed, although careful consideration needs to be given to the practicality and feasibility of their collection. Many States have limited resources for management of data, and indicators need to be amenable to both collection and analysis. It is important to recognize the positive role that children themselves can contribute to the monitoring process.[52] They can be involved in helping define the indicators, as respondents in the collection of data and as researchers.

## Meaningful intersectoral collaboration

The Committee on the Rights of the Child calls on all States to develop national plans of action that embody strategies for the implementation of rights-based education systems.[53] The fulfilment of children's rights to and within education at all levels, including the early years of development, can only be achieved by a comprehensive and multisectoral approach involving legislative and policy reform, collaboration and partnerships, and commitment of resources. Although direct responsibility for education usually lies in an individual governmental department, the factors that contribute to its realization necessitate action on the part of the whole of government. A coordinated mechanism is needed for planning, budgeting and implementation across government departments and at all educational levels including, for example:

- **Education** – having overall responsibility for children's education and the training of teachers.

- **Finance** – ensuring that an appropriate commitment of government resources are allocated to achieve the goals established in the education strategy.
- **Water and sanitation** – ensuring appropriate and equitable access to safe drinking water, hygiene education and sanitation in schools, and eliminating the barriers to girls' education associated with lack of privacy and appropriate facilities.

## The impact of a human rights-based analysis on education policy

In Chile, a rights-based analysis of education highlighted distinct areas of concern of which the Government had previously been unaware. The Government had introduced educational reforms and was collecting data on school enrolment in secondary schools in order to monitor its progress on the Education for All commitments. Because national coverage was around 65 per cent, increasing access and retention was not defined as a key policy issue for secondary education. The United Nations Children's Fund undertook a more comprehensive rights-based analysis, which showed that 70 per cent of students who dropped out were from the poorest families. The reasons were partly economic, with young people needing to work to support their families, and partly related to the failure of the schools to meet the needs of the young people due to an irrelevant curriculum and inadequate pedagogic practices. The rigidity of schools and lack of flexibility to accommodate the needs of different students was also a factor.

The critical difference was that the rights-based analysis:

- Disaggregated the data to reveal inequalities and social exclusion against low-income groups.
- Took a broader view of the right to education including quality and outcomes.
- Built in opportunities to consult with students themselves to incorporate their perspectives into the analysis, findings and subsequent strategies for action.

Access to this kind of information enables the development of more effective and targeted policies to remove barriers and reduce discrimination. In fact, the Government subsequently redefined the policy priorities at this level, passed a law to incorporate secondary school as part of compulsory education, modified the school finance system to provide additional resources to high schools in poor areas and created several compensatory programmes to reduce dropout by tackling specific issues, such as opportunity costs for families, psychosocial problems at school and pedagogic challenges at classroom level.

**Source:** Bellei, Cristián, 'Educación Secundaria como Derecho Universal: Cooperación de UNICEF en Chile 1998–2002', Santiago, July 2003, internal UNICEF document.

- **Public works** – addressing issues of inclusion, such as consideration of access for children with disabilities, in designing and building schools.
- **Health** – introducing programmes of health care, health education, nutrition and feeding into schools to improve children's health and their capacity for learning. Health departments also need to be involved in the development of curricula related to life skills, HIV and AIDS, reproductive health and other vital concerns. Health systems can also support early stimulation programmes through parent training.
- **Child protection** – ensuring that appropriate child protection legislation and policies are developed and implemented in and around schools.
- **Social development, welfare and protection** – introducing poverty reduction schemes to increase enrolment, reduce child labour, and improve attendance and attainment.
- **Employment** – addressing the reduction in child labour through the involvement of government departments responsible for legislation and policy on working children, health and safety at work, and employment conditions and rights.
- **Culture and sports** – expanding learning opportunities that reinforce and complement school-based programmes.

## Effective partnerships

States need to build partnerships with all key organizations and institutions that have an impact on the right to education. Collaboration, for example, is needed with non-governmental organizations, teacher unions, the private sector, traditional leaders and religious groups to enlist their support and expertise in building capacity to ensure the right of education for all children throughout the life cycle and in a wider range of learning spaces.

Although the State has the primary obligation to provide education for all children, non-governmental organizations and other civil society partners make a vital contribution to education in many countries, mobilizing public demand and expanding participation. Recognition needs to be afforded to the role of the non-government education sector in creating additional learning spaces and opportunities that complement the school process and are linked to specific actions, for example, violence prevention, elimination of child labour, and promotion of peer-to-peer relationships and partnerships. At the same time, however, there may be a stigma attached to children who are not part of the formal education system and the qualifications it offers. Assessment of the contribution of the non-government sector is needed in order to explore how the systems can better complement each other and how to strengthen opportunities for children to transfer from that sector into government schools to allow them to take state examinations and certificates.

## Collaboration with the non-formal education sector to achieve the Education for All goals

In Ethiopia, Pact's NGO Sector Enhancement Initiative for basic alternative education sought to work with the Government to put in place policies and directives that would allow for alternative basic education to be included as a means of achieving the Education for All goals, including a directive to permit the transfer of children from alternative to formal basic education schools. Thirteen non-governmental organizations were supported to establish and manage 165 alternative basic education centres. The approach employs community ownership – including dialogue, action planning, management of the centres and a cost-share plan – customized curricular materials and substantial involvement of local government. A strong emphasis is placed on reaching out-of-school children in pastoral and food insecure peripheral areas.

The programme reached 25,000 out-of-school children who otherwise would not have had a chance to receive an education. In particular, it used flexible hours to meet the needs of agrarian communities, increased retention rates and brought girls' attendance to parity with boys'. A subsequent five-year cooperative agreement between Pact and the United States Agency for International Development is intended to reach a further 275,000 children who lack access to primary education facilities with quality non-formal education services. Through training, the programme will strengthen the capacity of 600 education personnel in 70 education offices to manage both formal and non-formal education programmes.

**Sources:** Pact Ethiopia, *IMPact*, no. 23, July-December 2004, p. 5; United States Agency for International Development, 'USAID Invests $11.6 million to Expand Non-formal Primary Education Services in Ethiopia', press release, 26 January 2005.

# ESTABLISHING A ROBUST LEGISLATIVE FRAMEWORK

Educational rights – consistent with human rights principles as they pertain to access, quality and respect – need to be embedded in the legislative framework. They should be clearly acknowledged as entitlements for which governments are responsible and that individuals can claim and, if necessary, have enforced through the courts. Such legislation not only needs to take into account the international obligations that an individual State has in respect to fulfilment of that particular right via incorporation into domestic law, but it should also address the removal of direct and indirect barriers that impede access. The specific legislative measures required will vary according to the different country context but may include the following:

- Education as a right for all children.
- Elimination of discrimination.
- Minimum standards.
- Best interests of the child.
- An inclusive framework.
- Elimination of child labour.
- Birth registration.
- Participation rights.
- Prohibition of all forms of violence against children.

## Education as a right for all children

Legislation must ensure the entitlement of all children to compulsory primary education. In some countries, this is provided in the constitution, and consideration may be given to amending constitutions to introduce a universal right to education where it is not provided for. In India, for instance, the Constitution was amended via the 93rd Constitutional Amendment to provide universal, free and compulsory primary education to all children between the ages of 6 and 14.[54] Even in 2004, however, at least 25 countries still had no specified age for compulsory education.[55] Wherever possible, consideration should also be given to including entitlement to secondary education as a longer-term goal. Consideration should also be given to introducing an entitlement to care and education during the early years with family involvement.

## Elimination of discrimination

States need to undertake a review of existing legislation to ensure that no direct or indirect discriminations in the law impede the right to education for all children. Legislative action to protect those children vulnerable to discrimination should include:

- **Gender** – eliminating laws that allow girls to marry before the compulsory school-leaving age or allow differences in school-leaving ages or numbers of years of compulsory education for girls and boys.
- **Children with disabilities** – ensuring the right to education on an equal basis with other children, including access to the same curriculum and opportunities to enter public examinations, and eliminating laws that differentiate between children who are deemed to be 'educable' and 'non-educable'.
- **Ethnic minority and indigenous children** – ensuring equitable levels of funding, quality, access, teachers' qualifications or pay for all schools, whether integrated or separate; elimination of imposed racial segregation in schools;[56] and equitable access for children who are refugees or seeking asylum.[57]
- **Children in institutions** – satisfying the legal right to education of such children on an equal basis with others and, wherever possible, in the community in local schools, including children in penal and residential institutions and those in long-stay hospitals.
- **Children who are pregnant or parents** – guaranteeing their right to attend schools.
- **Children with specific health impairments or limiting conditions** – enabling their access to school.

Because many children experience multiple types of discrimination together with poverty-related exclusion from education, the Special Rapporteur for Education has recommended "merging the conventional focus on legislative measures for the elimination of discrimination with measures aimed at overcoming poverty-based exclusion."[58]

## Minimum standards

Minimum levels of qualification need to be established for teachers at all levels of the education system, and the same standards applied to schools in both urban and rural areas. Full-time education should be defined in terms of a specific number of hours per week and weeks per year and laid down in statute in order to establish the exact entitlement of children. There has to be a commitment to defining the maximum desired number of pupils per teacher in a class, and to introducing a time frame for working towards achieving that ratio in all classes. It can also be helpful to introduce requirements to involve local community members on school governing bodies to strengthen community support and ownership, and promote accountability and transparency. In particular, girls' attendance can be encouraged by increasing the involvement of women. For example, there could be a statutory obligation to ensure that women make up a given proportion of the school governing body.

## Best interests of the child

The principle that the best interests of the child shall be the primary consideration in all actions concerning him or her needs to be introduced into all relevant legislation, including in educational laws.

## An inclusive framework

Anti-discrimination legislation that introduces a prohibition on policies, practices and actions that directly or indirectly discriminate will not be sufficient to end all forms of exclusion and segregation. For example, separate schooling systems for children with disabilities are often sustained without breaching non-discrimination laws. It is, therefore, possible to go further and introduce a positive obligation to promote inclusive educational environments. Legislation can establish a commitment to inclusion, introduce requirements on education authorities to take all necessary measures to ensure that no groups of children are excluded and that the barriers that may impede their access are removed, create incentives to promote socially inclusive school environments, and design and implement affirmative action or positive discrimination programmes.

## Elimination of child labour

Ultimately, the elimination of child labour is a prerequisite for the realization of children's education rights. Evidence indicates that child workers, even when they attend school, tend to achieve lower learning outcomes than children who are not working.[59] A range of legislative reforms can be introduced to begin the process of ending child labour. Many countries currently fail to synchronize their legislation to ensure there is consistency between the minimum age for full-time work and the school-leaving age in line with International Labour Organization (ILO) Convention 138.[60] It is important to ensure that these align. Without such legislation, children can legitimately be employed at an age when they should be in full-time education. The introduction of a minimum wage, applicable equally to children, will serve to discourage employers from using children as a cheap source of labour. Legislation must be introduced to prohibit the use of children in hazardous, harmful and exploitative forms of work and bring countries in line with the standards of the Convention on the Rights of the Child (article 32) and relevant ILO conventions.[61]

## Birth registration

For many children, the lack of a birth certificate results in the denial of a place in school. Despite the clear obligation in the Convention on the Rights of the Child to ensure that every child is registered at birth, up to 50 million births were unregistered in 2003 – 36 per cent of all births that year.[62] Many poor children face this problem, but children with disabilities are disproportionately vulnerable to non-registration. Universal registration is also essential for providing governments with accurate data with which to plan for building facilities, training educators, and the fulfilment of children's educational and other rights.

Lack of parental documentation, inability to pay the fees, lack of access to the registration systems, parental illiteracy and lack of understanding of the significance of holding a birth certificate all contribute to the failure to register children's births. States need to introduce a universal requirement to register every birth and can support the process by, for example, ending the legal requirement that parents present their own identity papers and, until there is universal registration, removing any requirement to provide evidence of birth as a condition of enrolment in school. In addition to legislation, strategies to increase rates of birth registration include mobilization campaigns to increase public demand, elimination or reduction of registration fees and simplification of registration procedures. Mobile registrars have been set up in rural areas of Colombia, for example, where low levels of birth registration have been identified.[63]

## Participation rights

The right of children to express views and have them given due weight in respect of their education will never be fully realized without the establishment of an underpinning legal framework. Legislation needs to be introduced requiring schools to establish democratic bodies run by students, such as school councils, through which they can represent their concerns. This has been done, for example, in several European and Latin American countries. In addition, it would be valuable to establish an entitlement for children to be consulted, through the school system, on aspects of educational policy at the national level.

## Prohibition of all forms of violence against children

Legislation is needed to prohibit all forms of physical and humiliating punishment of children in school.[64] This needs to be undertaken within a framework of legislation to end all forms of violence against children, including in the home, and to provide effective mechanisms for complaint by children when the law is broken.[65] *The World Report on Violence Against Children* provides detailed recommendations for action to prevent violence against children in school.[66]

# DEVELOPING RIGHTS-BASED EDUCATION POLICIES

In the context of the broader conducive political and economic environment, States need to develop specific education policies aimed at realizing the right to education for every child. Measures need to be introduced that address the provision of education throughout childhood, ensure the quality of that education and provide learning environments that are respectful of the human rights of children.

## Policies to ensure access to education

First and foremost, States must invest in the infrastructure to create learning environments and opportunities for the education of every child. Provision of schools, teachers, books and equipment is a fundamental prerequisite of education. But if the right of every child is to be realized, that provision needs to be sufficiently flexible and inclusive to address the learning needs of all children. It also needs to be sensitive to and respectful of the different circumstances of children, particularly the most marginalized. This will necessitate action to remove the multiple barriers that impede children's access to education.

### Adopting a life-cycle approach

The right to an education that brings about their optimum development requires investment in children throughout their childhood. In terms of national policy and planning, a life-cycle approach based on the human rights of children necessitates action beyond the basic provision of universal access to primary education to include pre- and post-primary provision.

### Rights-based, integrated and multisectoral strategies for early childhood

Strategies for early childhood that are effectively coordinated, comprehensive and backed by effective information and monitoring systems, produce the best and most sustainable outcomes for children.[67] Efforts need to target the most marginalized children, to overcome the educational disadvantage associated with poverty and social exclusion. Parents should also be "consulted and involved" in the planning of services to empower them to fulfil their children's rights.[68] Efforts should be made to increase the competencies of parents to increase the child's readiness and ease the transitioning process. Integrated approaches are needed that involve: strengthening the capacities of families and other caregivers; mobilizing community demand for the skills, knowledge and services essential for ensuring children have the best start in life; coordinating and integrating maternal health interventions with those focused on early childhood to enhance mutual benefits; and investing in programmes for psychosocial care and early learning. Integrated approaches to early childhood are also essential in emergency situations, particularly in complex emergencies, because children are exposed to increased risks and families' coping strategies have been diminished.

### Primary education

A free primary school place needs to be made available for every child entitled to it, including those in situations of risk (see 'Situations of risk', p. 61). Mechanisms should also be developed to ensure availability of education for marginalized groups of children – for example, working children, children living on the street, children in rural communities and children in institutions – either in schools in the local community or, where it is not possible for a child to leave the institution, in the institution itself.

### Commitment to secondary and vocational education

Clearly, countries are at very different stages with regard to the provision of secondary education, but it needs to be established as a priority goal in the overall commitment to progressive realization of education rights.

## A multisector approach to promoting the right to education for children living and working on the street

A multisector approach adopted in Burundi to extend the right to education for children living and working on the street has enabled more than 2,000 such children to attend primary schools. Some of them have even reached secondary-level education. The programme 'Education for street children' aims to provide access to basic education and to support the Government of Burundi in attaining its objective of education for all. It relies on a widespread partnership (Ministries, UN Agencies, NGOs, private companies) and stresses long-term pedagogical support as well as assistance for families and host centres through regular visits to underscore the necessity of education, provide assistance in managing supplies given by the World Food Programme and elaborate income-generating activities.

**Source:** UNESCO information based on interviews.

### Collaboration by providers across the age spectrum

Collaboration is essential if children are to achieve the maximum benefit from each stage of their education. This involves effective planning for the transfer by children from preschool to primary and on to secondary education, a coherent approach to the development of curricula, consistent commitment to rights-based principles in education at all stages, and ongoing provision of information and support to parents and children.

### Providing available and accessible schools

#### Identification of the eligible preschool and school-aged population

Accurate information on the preschool and school-aged population in each district or locality is needed to ensure that the availability of places, trained teachers and educational resources is consistent with the size of that population. The process of mapping can be undertaken in partnership with local non-governmental organizations, community members, traditional leaders, religious organizations and parent groups. Efforts need to be made to include the less visible children, such as children with disabilities, children of migrant and domestic workers and children with specific health impairments. In communities where families deny the existence of a child with a disability because of associated stigma or shame, the involvement of organizations of persons with disabilities or parents of children with disabilities in the process of data collection has been effective.[69] Child-to-child approaches to mapping have also helped raise awareness.[70] As noted earlier, birth registration is an important factor in building accurate records of child populations, and schools can play a key role by providing a site for this.

### Child-seeking and participatory mapping

Even with the declaration of free primary education, an estimated 1.7 million children are still not attending school in Kenya. Building on the principles of child participation, a child-to-child census was designed as a mechanism to seek them out, determine why they are out of school and bring them back in. School children and their teachers were trained to go into their neighbourhoods to ask these children why they were not in school. The key reasons included poverty, lack of school uniforms, domestic work and distance from school. Solutions were discussed, and in one of the three pilot districts, around 7,000 out of the 9,000 identified out-of-school children – half of them girls – were brought back into school through community dialogue and support. This strategy was employed as part of the child-friendly school approach, which demands that schools actively seek out and welcome those who are excluded for any reason. This approach highlighted the power and potential of children's participation to such an extent that it has been recognized as a key element and included in the national education sector plan.

Source: Kenya Country Office Annual Report, 2004, internal United Nations Children's Fund document.

### Location of schools

Consideration needs to be given to ensure that schools are accessible to all children irrespective of age, disability, gender, caste, ethnicity or other factors. Consultation with different members of the community can be vital in identifying potential barriers to access. For example, it can be helpful to establish small multigrade or multi-age schools in remote rural areas. Satellite schools have been one approach to addressing the difficulties faced by young children, especially girls, travelling long distances to school. In Burkina Faso, a network of satellite schools has been developed that provides for the first three grades and allows the youngest children to gain their first experience of school close to their own villages. This system has achieved substantial benefits for children, with a retention rate of 95 per cent and significantly improved performance rates in writing, reading and arithmetic skills.[71] Community learning centres can also provide an effective educational environment for young children who cannot travel to an early childhood centre or a school at a distance from home, or for out-of-school children.[72]

## The importance of consulting children

In one village in India, the World Bank and local authorities funded a new primary school. However, a year after its completion, the children were still not attending. When asked why, they explained that there was an invisible boundary around the village that marked the limit of safe travel on foot for children from lower castes, and that the school was located outside this boundary. Had the planners consulted with them, the children would have been able to explain this and the school would have been located in a more appropriate site.

**Source:** Socknat, James, Asia Technical Division, World Bank, cited in van Reisen, M. *Invisible Children?*, Save the Children, 2002.

### Provision of schools and other learning environments

Sufficient school facilities must be provided for all eligible children. From the outset, account needs to be taken of the specific access needs of all children, including those with disabilities. The physical design and resources available in school can serve as barriers to inclusion, and it is far harder to redress inaccessible design after schools have been built. Governments need to consult with the community in the design and construction of schools. The needs of children with different physical abilities, as well as the needs of both girls and boys, should be reflected in the design of all equipment and resources, as well as play and sports facilities in schools and surrounding community spaces. Schools must ensure that hygiene and sanitation facilities are appropriate for both boys and girls – clean water, proper toilet facilities and privacy, particularly for girls – and take account of any religious requirements. In addition, some children will require aids such as wheelchairs if they are to be able to attend school.

### Teaching and learning materials

Schools are not accessible unless they have adequate educational materials. Appropriate measures need to be introduced to review the total equipment requirements. If all children are to have equal opportunities to learn, attention has to be paid to specific needs. Children with severe visual impairments, for example, will need Braille books and teachers trained to teach them to read. In addition, measures need to be taken to ensure that the whole curriculum is available in Braille and that it is published in time for each academic year. Children with severe hearing impairments will need teachers or assistants who can communicate in sign language. Children whose first language is not the school's medium of instruction need materials in their own language, as well as access to bilingual teaching. Consideration should be given to whether such items as textbooks, notebooks, pencils, chalk and chalkboards are manufactured in the country and, if not, whether there are taxation and trade policies that will affect their availability. Attention also needs to be paid to whether the State needs capacity-building assistance to enable it to produce the items in the country.

Situations of risk

Every effort needs to be made to restore education to children in situations of risk including extreme poverty, conflict, health crises (including HIV and AIDS) and emergencies. Although the same principles must apply – the right of every child to access to quality education in which her or his human rights are respected – the strategies for providing education in emergencies differ. One important learning point is that a crisis or emergency situation can provide an opportunity to build a better education system than existed before. It can offer an opportunity to address social exclusion and discrimination, mobilize community support and action, and involve more women. The United Nations Children's Fund and the United Nations Educational, Scientific and Cultural Organization have provided programme guidance on how to restore education to children in emergencies and produced a number of publications highlighting the strategies that have been developed and implemented successfully.[73] The Inter-Agency Network for Education in Emergencies (INEE), which was conceived during the World Education Forum's 'Strategy Session on Education in Emergencies' held in Dakar, has also evolved as a resource to improve understanding and effectiveness in ensuring the right to education in emergencies.[74]

### Encouraging duty bearers to fulfil obligations in situations of conflict

In 2002, children in Papua New Guinea were being denied the right to education in 'no-go' zones controlled by rebels fighting for secession. The United Nations Children's Fund negotiated with ex-combatants, village chiefs, women's groups and other stakeholders to argue for the importance of protecting children's access to education. Permission was subsequently given by the rebel commanders to implement education programmes in a limited number of zones, and teachers were provided with specialized training before returning. The programme was so successful it was extended to other zones and laid a firm foundation for the recovery of the education system.

Source: United Nations Children's Fund, *The State of the World's Children 2005: Childhood under threat*, UNICEF, New York, 2004, p. 59.

## Fulfilling education rights in humanitarian disasters

Emergencies can provide opportunities to improve schools/learning spaces and enhance child-friendliness. In Iran, a devastating earthquake killed 30 per cent of the students in one city and one third of their teachers. More than 130 schools were destroyed, and many of those remaining were damaged beyond repair. Three weeks later, in order to ensure a return to normalcy for children, schools were officially reopened – first in open-air spaces, then in tents and containers. Support for access included provision of tents and 'mobile' education and recreation; establishment of a tracking system for out-of-school children; tools for data collection, management and analysis; and establishment of learning spaces linked to early childhood development centres, and non-formal education and recreation centres. Advocacy and technical support were provided for a review of national school design, with a view to promoting healthy and safe girl-friendly environments, including water and sanitation; playgrounds or sports areas; and the involvement of children and the community in school design and construction.

Interventions in the country to improve learning quality have supported advocacy for girl-friendly schools as a package at policy and school levels; teacher support, including psychosocial support and services; extra-curricular courses (psychosocial education, life skills, hygiene education); review of educational and recreational materials; participatory, child-centred and gender-sensitive teaching methods; children's participation in schools (clubs, school governance); enhanced community involvement in planning, management, and monitoring and evaluation of educational activities (school management); implementation of 'catch-up' classes; and school environments and learning materials to meet the needs of disabled children.

**Source:** Iran Country Office Annual Report, 2006, internal United Nations Children's Fund document.

## Removing the economic barriers to education

Measures to remove the economic barriers to education need to be embedded in the annual action plans of national poverty reduction strategy papers.[75] Some examples are the abolition of school fees and charges, and the provision of stipends and cash transfers.

### Abolition of school fees and charges

Compulsory education cannot be implemented unless it is provided to all free of charge. The continuing imposition of fees has been challenged from both a human rights and a poverty-reduction perspective.[76] Fees are common in primary education in many developing countries faced with resource constraints and "represent perhaps 20 per cent of all education spending, and as much as 30 per cent in Africa."[77] Direct tuition fees and textbook charges are less common than community contributions, parent-teacher associations' dues and compulsory uniforms.[78] Both direct and indirect costs may prevent poorer children from exercising their right to education. In fact, experience from various countries shows that the abolition of fees has been successful in creating significant increases in enrolment and in improving equitable access to education.[79]

However, the abolition of school fees and other charges is not a panacea. The consequent increased enrolment can lead to a reduction in quality due to overcrowding and lack of textbooks and adequately trained teachers, leading in a few years to falling enrolment and higher drop-out rates. For some marginalized or vulnerable communities – for example, children in households affected by HIV/AIDS – abolition of fees alone is insufficient to overcome the barriers to education. Furthermore, abolition necessarily results in rising expenditures for governments that need to be budgeted for in terms of fee replacement and quality inputs. Finally, more rapid and efficient management and logistical measures are needed to address the surge in enrolment in a timely and sustained fashion.

## An approach to abolition of fees

Fees cannot simply be abolished without consideration of whether, and how, they should be replaced by an alternative source of income. When fees contribute to operational effectiveness, or even perceived quality, simply abolishing them without replacement can result in serious deterioration of the education system, as shown in a number of countries. Uganda prepared better, or at least adapted more quickly to what was needed, increasing the recurrent budget for primary education from 9 per cent of total education spending in 1996 to 19 per cent by 1999, and reducing the subsidies for higher education.

The case of Uganda illustrates what needs to be in place to support elimination of user fees. The Government's broad consultations with the World Bank and other external donors on the development of an investment and policy framework for education to close the financing gap resulted in a comprehensive and systematic response by the Government, increased external resources, and improved sector management and transparency at the school level.

**Source:** Kattan, Raja Bentaouet, and Nicholas Burnett, *User Fees In Primary Education*, World Bank, Washington, D.C., 2004, pp. 23, 29.

Several strategies thus need to be put in place to address the challenges of fee abolition. First of all, the commitment to abolition needs to be integrated into wider education programmes and budgets and accompanied by careful planning. A phased-in approach can reduce the technical and financing challenges. Sources of revenue to replace the fees and increase quality inputs can come from shifting spending from other sectors, shifting cost recovery to higher educational levels, improving efficiency of education spending and donor support. Finally, targeted interventions, such as cash transfers, can play an important role in reaching the hard core of poor, excluded and vulnerable children.[80]

## Stipends and cash transfers

The impact of sending a child to school may be the loss of his or her earnings or contribution to the domestic chores in the home. There is frequently a conflict between the financial needs of the family and the individual child's right to education. Poor families will often need incentives or help to offset the associated costs of their child's education. There is evidence of the efficacy of food-for-education programmes, as well as stipend and cash transfer schemes.[81] The Food for Education programme of the Government of Bangladesh, for example, has significantly increased enrolment and attendance and reduced drop-out rates for primary-school-age children.[82] Unconditional cash transfers have been applied with considerable effect in South and southern Africa.[83] Conditional cash transfers, where payment is linked to attendance at school, have been shown to lead to positive outcomes for children in Latin America but have been less popular in Africa, perhaps because the quality of education is so poor that the benefits of the imposition of such conditionalities are doubtful.[84]

To be effective, these programmes need to be integrated into comprehensive packages of context-specific social protection interventions and must involve partnerships including governments, non-governmental organizations, communities, the private sector and donors to support delivery. Questions of sustainability, corruption in the delivery process and stigma for beneficiaries need to be addressed. It is also important that such schemes are viewed as a social contract between governments and citizens and not just as part of a donor-driven initiative to be abandoned when the project cycle ends.

## Promoting inclusion and eliminating discrimination

A rights-based inclusive approach requires a national policy framework that addresses the access and learning needs of all children and supports the need for changes in respect of the culture, policies and practices in schools.

## What is inclusion?

"UNESCO views inclusion as '*a dynamic approach of responding positively to pupil diversity and of seeing individual differences not as problems, but as opportunities for enriching learning.*'

"Therefore, the move towards inclusion is not simply a technical or organizational change but also a movement with a clear philosophy. In order for inclusion to be implemented effectively, countries need to define a set of inclusive principles together with practical ideas to guide the transition towards policies addressing inclusion in education. The principles of inclusion that are set out in various international declarations can be used as a foundation. These then can be interpreted and adapted to the context of individual countries."

**Source:** United Nations Educational, Scientific and Cultural Organization, *Guidelines for Inclusion: Ensuring Access to Education for All*, UNESCO, Paris, 2005, p. 12.

A multisector and cross-departmental approach is required, including attention to:

- **Sensitization on the rights of all children to education**: National campaigns and information dissemination are necessary to challenge many of the cultural barriers and discriminatory attitudes and beliefs that serve to impede access to education.
- **Parental and family support**: Parents need to be supported to promote both their willingness and capacity to ensure their children's attendance at school.
- **An inclusive ethos and environment**: Schools need to be provided with policies and guidance on how to create learning environments that respond to, and value, the differing needs of children. They need to promote a culture of respect for difference and introduce approaches to support all children, irrespective of gender, language, ethnicity or disability.
- **A flexible structure and timetable**: Schools should adapt to children rather than the other way round, especially during the early years and through the first grades of primary school. It is necessary to explore options for a less rigid and more inclusive approach to the organization of schools, if certain groups of children – including children affected by AIDS, temporary migrants, children affected by the agricultural economy and those involved in domestic labour – are to realize their right to education.

However, flexibility should not extend to the exclusion of certain groups of children from the curriculum being offered to others. Offering shorter alternative curricula for working children or those with disabilities can serve to discriminate and to limit their future opportunities. Of course, children are entitled to protection from economic exploitation and from any work that interferes with their health, education or development.[85] The first priority must be to ensure that children are not forced into work that prohibits their access to and opportunity to benefit from education. Until this goal is realized, working children are entitled to an education that accommodates the competing demands on their time.

All efforts to increase the enrolment and attendance of girls in school need to address the deep-seated and widespread cultural norms and values that impede their access to education. Millennium Development Goal 3 – to eliminate gender disparity in education by 2015 – will not be achieved in all regions without a multifaceted approach to removing the barriers faced by girls in exercising their right to education without discrimination (*see box on page 67*).

The special needs of orphans also have to be addressed. Orphans in a number of countries across Africa have been found to be disadvantaged in terms of continuity of schooling and appropriate grade for age. Analysis from eastern Africa in 2003 shows that double orphans (those who have lost both parents) aged 6–10 are half as likely to be at the correct educational level as children who are not orphans, and by age 11–14, that figure rises to two thirds.[86] Targeted measures are needed to ensure their equal right to education.

## Policies to provide quality education

Quality in education can only be achieved through the development of child-friendly learning environments that are dedicated to a holistic approach to children's development. This means addressing children's multiple rights, using strategies that build links between the school and the family and community. Child-friendly learning environments seek not only to equip children with basic learning skills but also to enable them to take control of their lives and to promote justice, democracy, peace and tolerance. The child-friendly learning concept promotes child-seeking, child-centred, gender-sensitive, inclusive, community-involved, protective and healthy approaches to schooling and out-of-school education. These approaches are intended to increase the learning effectiveness, efficiency and reach of education systems and to enable all children to realize their right to learn. Child-friendly schools have been applied in many settings around the world in formal and non-formal education, early child development and educational responses to emergencies.

## A multisectored approach to tackling gender discrimination

Effective strategies to achieve equality for girls and boys in access to education include:

- Increased numbers of female teachers, including, where necessary, quotas for the proportion of female teachers in any school.

- Review of the curriculum to eliminate male bias and insensitivity to women and girls, render it more relevant and appropriate to their lives, and challenge and question traditional hierarchies in gender relations.

- Introduction of satellite schools or other forms of schools in all localities.

- Provision of appropriate hygiene and sanitation facilities in all schools.

- Food-for-education programmes or cash transfers for enrolment of girls in primary and secondary education.

- Child protection strategies to address physical and sexual abuse in schools and ensure the safety of girls travelling to and from school.

- Sensitization of parents to encourage them to understand the value of girls' education.

- Training for teachers on gender equality.

- Promotion of early childhood and school programmes to promote a more equitable and healthy relationship between boys and girls.

- Support for the increased involvement of both mothers and fathers in school governing bodies through social mobilization programmes.

- Improved disaggregation of data on the basis of gender in order to enhance capacity to monitor progress in girls' participation in schools.

- Investment in such programmes as rural water supplies and improved roads and electricity to ease the workloads of women, thus increasing the opportunities for girls to be released into education.

The concept of a child-friendly school embodies all three dimensions of access, quality and respect addressed in this chapter. This section focuses on the specific issues relating to quality in respect of the curriculum, rights-based learning and assessment, support and training for teachers, and the creation of safe and healthy environments, as well as support to community involvement.

**Providing a broad, relevant and inclusive curriculum**

A nationally prescribed curriculum, compulsory for all schools and focused on fundamental knowledge and skills, is needed. It should address all aspects of children's development and provide an appropriate balance between study and play, consistent with their evolving capacities and needs at all levels – preschool, primary and secondary.

The right to education means acquiring basic numeracy and literacy skills. In addition, the curriculum needs to include a broad range of subjects, including science, humanities, the arts, sports and life skills. Human rights education is essential in all learning environments, although to date it has been given too little attention in many countries.[87] It can be taught as a discrete subject but can also be incorporated in other subjects – for example, in geography to explore the issue of unequal access to resources, in languages to explore the implications of how language can exclude some groups, and in science to examine the impact of environmental pollution and the right to health. However, human rights education cannot be limited to the taught curriculum. The learning environment, educational content, and teaching and learning processes should all reflect human rights principles. The UN General Assembly has adopted a resolution for a World Programme for Human Rights Education, which started in 2005. This is accompanied by a Plan of Action, prepared by the Office of the United Nations High Commissioner for Human Rights (OHCHR), in cooperation with UNESCO, that will focus on primary and secondary school systems in its first three years (*see Appendix V, page 128*).

The curriculum must also be relevant to the lives of children. It is therefore important to consider involving teachers and students in its development. There needs to be some flexibility in the curriculum to allow schools and early childhood settings to adapt it to reflect the interests, concerns and needs of the local environment, and to allow the interests of children to be accommodated and valued. It is, however, imperative that flexibility should not be used to justify a reduced or minimalist curriculum.

The right to education also means learning for life. The curriculum must be aimed at ensuring that essential life skills are learned by every child and that no child leaves school without being equipped to face the challenges he or she can expect to be

## Inclusive education

To support children with disabilities in Viet Nam, Catholic Relief Services and the Center for Special Education of the National Institute of Education Science began piloting small projects in 1995 that focused on preschool and awareness-raising in selected target communities. The project was later expanded with funding from the United States Agency for International Development. It provides technical and financial support in order to integrate disabled children into mainstream classrooms and supports the provision of community-based inclusive education services and rehabilitation.

Over a five-year period (1998–2003), the project focused on the following major activities:

- Development of training materials and textbooks on inclusive education.
- Organizing training courses on teaching children with disabilities for in-service teachers of preschools and primary schools and pre-service teachers of teacher training colleges.
- Increasing awareness of disabilities in general and the unique needs of children who experience disabilities.
- Strengthening community support.

The initiative works at both the preschool and primary school level. Early identification and integration of children with disabilities tends to improve their level of rehabilitation, enhance social integration and ensure that they are included in classrooms with other children of their same age. In addition, the project provides a resource centre for parents, teachers and community workers involved in the rehabilitation activities. Efforts are made to integrate the activities of raising community awareness, coordinating community services, teacher/parent training, and adapting curriculum and low-cost teaching materials.

**Source:** United Nations Children's Fund, *Inclusive Education Initiatives for Children with Disabilities: Lessons from the East Asia and Pacific region*, UNICEF, Bangkok, March 2003, pp. 39–40.

confronted with in life. Those skills include "the ability to make well-balanced decisions; to resolve conflicts in a non-violent manner; and to develop a healthy lifestyle, good social relationships and responsibility, critical thinking, creative talents, and other abilities which give children the tools needed to pursue their options in life."[88]

The curriculum, textbooks and learning materials need to be appropriate for all students and seek to promote and respect diversity. States are required to provide an education for all children on the basis of equality of opportunity. To achieve this objective, it is essential that all children are rendered visible in the curriculum and that no discrimination or prejudice is explicitly or implicitly reflected in it – whether on the basis of gender, ethnicity, class, caste, language, culture or religion. As noted earlier, the curriculum also needs to include alternative forms of communication for children with disabilities, particularly those who have severe hearing and visual impairments, such as learning of Braille, and orientation and mobility skills. Children who are not learning in their own language need appropriate assistance.[89] The curriculum also needs to be developed with regard to children's evolving capacities.

**Developing rights-based learning and assessment processes**

Measures are needed to introduce rights-based learning environments in which the role of teachers and parents is defined in terms of inspiring children's confidence in what they can achieve through positive reinforcement, encouragement and active engagement in their own learning. Children need to be helped to acquire skills in analysing, investigating, creating and applying knowledge if they are to achieve their optimum potential. It is important to recognize that children have different aptitudes and abilities and cannot all learn at the same pace. Their capacities do not evolve uniformly with age; rather, their circumstances and individual experiences will affect their development.[90] Different children will need differing levels of support, display differing levels of confidence and have differing capacities to support other children. Classroom environments, and teaching and learning resources, need to enhance a participatory approach to learning, with appropriate tools and resources to reflect these differences.

Expected learning outcomes should be established for each grade. However, it is not appropriate to punish or blame children who do not conform to these standards, which should be used to identify where additional support or encouragement is needed. Teachers need to acknowledge the differences between children and explore ways of capitalizing on the opportunities these provide. Children can work together in groups of mixed or the same ability. Older or more able students can be appointed as mentors to help those who have missed some schooling or need additional help. Evidence shows that these approaches benefit both more and less able children.[91]

## A rights-respecting model of education.

The Escuela Nueva (new school), an innovative rural school reform in Colombia, was established to address disparities in educational opportunities for rural children. The model is essentially a refinement and expansion of ideas from the 'unitary schools' project – designed in the 1960s to allow one teacher to supervise several grades – and was developed by a group of rural primary school teachers. They created learning guides with self-instructional activities for all the basic subjects and all five grade levels. As a result of recognition from the Ministry of Education, and with funding and support from the United Nations Children's Fund and the United States Agency for International Development, the programme was being implemented in 500 primary schools in rural areas by 1976.

The Escuela Nueva model creates opportunities for students and community members to have a degree of ownership over what could have been viewed as a reform imposed from outside. For example, the student government requires students to take on leadership roles and make decisions that affect their school environment. The self-instructional learning guides encourage active engagement of students in the learning process, often requiring them to work with their peers and explore their communities.

An evaluation of the Escuela Nueva model in 1987 concluded that its students scored significantly higher in third grade Spanish and math, and fifth grade Spanish than students in traditional rural schools. It also found that the students did better on civic values and self-esteem tests in both third and fifth grades. In 1989, there was a mass expansion of the programme, which has led to great variations among schools with the Escuela Nueva name. However, a 1999 evaluation still provides evidence that there was more active learning and group work, with more focus on student creativity and written and oral expression in these schools.

Source: Kline, Rachel, 'A Model for Improving Rural Schools: Escuela Nueva in Colombia and Guatemala', *Current Issues in Comparative Education*, vol. 2, no. 2, April 2002.

### Ensuring adequate training, support and respect for teachers

Creating a child-friendly school, based on respect for human rights, necessitates very different skills and styles from teaching in a traditional school, and teachers will need support in helping them understand, appreciate and implement the changes.

Teacher-training courses need to include a rights-based approach designed to build capacities and competencies on such issues as:

- Child-centred education.
- Evolving capacities of children.
- Learning through participation.
- Acting as a learning facilitator.
- Children's rights, including the principle of non-discrimination.
- Positive forms of discipline and class management.
- Teaching in inclusive environments.
- The participation of children at all levels in educational environments.

It is necessary to review both initial and in-service training and to develop a rolling programme to provide all teachers with training on the rights-based framework. In addition, it can be invaluable to build in a system of ongoing support for teachers – through, for example, fortnightly or monthly meetings of teachers in schools in the local community – to allow for opportunities to share ideas, challenges, strategies and solutions. UNESCO has developed a range of resources designed to help teachers create inclusive environments that a recent evaluation shows to have had significant impact on teacher capacity.[92]

It is imperative that, alongside a commitment to respect the rights of children, there is equal recognition afforded to the rights of teachers.[93] It is neither possible nor acceptable to demand that teachers respect children's rights when their own rights are violated and ignored. Ultimately, unless the rights of teachers are respected, a quality education for children cannot be achieved. Lack of support, low status, poor pay and inadequate training and supervision diminish the quality of teachers. There is widespread evidence among teachers in some countries of poor attendance, persistent lateness and low motivation.[94] Improved management, higher pay, effective appraisal systems, forums through which teachers can influence policy, acknowledgement of their concerns, and opportunities for them to identify their training and other needs would all contribute to improving morale and motivation and, in consequence, raise teaching standards. In terms of pay, for example, the Education for All FastTrack Initiative seeks to achieve an average annual teacher salary of 3.5 times the per capita gross domestic product by 2015.

## Introducing standards for child-friendly, safe and healthy learning environments

All learning environments, including those in the private and religious sector, must be underpinned by standards that ensure that the best interests of children are being promoted. Children cannot realize their right to education if they are frightened, hungry, ill or unsafe. This means that attention must be paid not only to the child's learning but also to the creation of safe, welcoming and healthy environments that promote children's emotional, psychological and physical well-being.

## Water and sanitation in child-friendly schools

In Nicaragua, the 'Healthy and Friendly Schools Initiative' was developed out of an integrated 'school sanitation and hygiene education' approach. The initiative aims to improve the school environment by addressing such issues as health, school hygiene, environmental sanitation and human rights in a comprehensive way, linked to quality learning. It is based on the idea that schools can help transform families and communities by promoting positive practices among pupils during their formative years. Participating schools have new hand-washing facilities and chlorinated water, as well as appropriate sanitary units (toilets or latrines) separated according to both age and sex, with smaller seats or toilets for preschool children, urinals for boys and one latrine adapted for children with disabilities. Life skills-based education and hygiene promotion have contributed to improved knowledge and the beginning of behavioural change.

This initiative is an example of child-friendly schools that have created broad-based partnerships among United Nations agencies` and different government sectors. It aims to ensure long-term sustainability by combining education, the promotion of suitable hygienic practices and improvements in school infrastructure – all with the active participation of the educational community and the local population, as well as the direct involvement of children.

Source: Nicaragua Country Office Annual Report, 2005, internal United Nations Children's Fund document.

### Providing a safe environment

States need to introduce minimum health and safety standards relating to all aspects of the learning environment. Schools should provide an appropriate quality of buildings and ensure safe water and appropriate sanitation facilities for both girls and boys. They need to ensure that all learning environments in and around the school are free from drugs, alcohol, tobacco or exposure to hazardous materials. Play areas must be designed to ensure opportunities for physical exercise and recreation, and school buildings and grounds must be checked to eliminate causes of potential injury. Furniture and equipment should be appropriate for the size and age of the children, and first-aid equipment must be available and properly maintained, and its application understood by staff. Efforts need to be made to address safety issues facing children in the school itself, as they travel to and from school, and even in the home. These standards must be capable of enforcement. In addition, an independent inspectorate needs to be established to assess the quality of education being provided and ensure that it complies with standards established in legislation and policy.

### Promoting child health

In a life-cycle approach, governments have an obligation to ensure adequate health care from the prenatal period and the first critical years of life, so that children are able to develop appropriately and are ready for school. Children are also entitled to protection from disorders or neglect that will impair their intellectual development – for example, lack of iodine or Vitamin A in the diet, which negatively affects cognitive development. Schools can play a key role in providing essential health services to children, integrating their learning with other essential services, particularly in communities where the social and economic conditions threaten children's well-being. They can provide a venue where children can receive food, nutrition, health checks, deworming, micronutrient supplementation, malaria prevention, and screening for visual and hearing impairments. Special attention should be given to orphans, children made vulnerable by AIDS and those living in highly violent situations. Schools can also contribute by listening to and detecting problems identified by children and referring them to appropriate services, either within or outside the school. In this way, they can serve as part of the child protection system through monitoring attendance and children's physical and emotional well-being.

Collaboration will be needed with health providers to explore the most effective models for the development of integrated services. Attention will need to be given to new methods of linking schools with other service providers and new ways of staffing and organizing schools, as well as innovative approaches to financing and managing them.[95] By becoming centres for community participation, schools and early learning centres can work more effectively in partnership with parents and other community members. Evidence also shows that schools have been the most effective – and cost-effective – means of protecting children and young people from HIV infection through becoming the centre of efforts to combat the disease and mitigate its impact.[96]

## Addressing the issue of AIDS awareness

In Lesotho, the development of child-friendly schools is undertaken within the broader vision to ensure access to and completion of a good quality education for all children. The overall goal is to assist in breaking the cycle of deprivation, poverty, discrimination and exclusion. With adult prevalence at around 23 per cent (21.9–24.7 per cent in 2006*), HIV is an issue of particular importance, especially for children and young adults, who have the highest proportion of new infections. Therefore, a specific feature of the child-friendly schools in Lesotho is the inclusion of AIDS awareness, protection issues and life skills acquisition. Important efforts for scaling up these activities are under way through the work of the National Curriculum and Development Centre to review and revise the national curriculum to ensure that it is responsive to HIV and AIDS, gender-sensitive and life skills-based, and through a collaborative effort by the Ministry of Education and Training and the Ministry of Health and Social Welfare to formulate a comprehensive school health policy to guide holistic approaches.

Source: Lesotho Country Office Annual Report, 2005, internal United Nations Children's Fund document. (*Joint United Nations Programme on HIV/AIDS, 2006 Report of the Global AIDS Epidemic, UNAIDS, Geneva, 2006, p. 18.)

### Ensuring community participation and accountability

A rights-based approach to education needs to be accountable to the stakeholders. The active engagement of local communities as stakeholders, participating in building, sustaining and monitoring provision, is an essential aspect of ensuring accountability and good governance. It is also necessary to introduce systems to provide access to justice when education rights are violated or denied. Complaints mechanisms need to be introduced to enable parents, children or other community members to challenge schools, local education authorities or governments when these fail to comply with the required standards.

## Policies to promote respect for human rights in schools

The World Programme for Human Rights Education Plan of Action has identified five essential components for achieving successful human rights education. Investment needs to be made in educational policies, policy implementation, the learning environment, teaching and learning, and professional development of teachers.[97] Promoting respect for human rights is not a matter simply, or even primarily, of the school curriculum. It cannot be taught in an environment where those rights are consistently violated. The principles must also permeate the ethos of the school, and the behaviour of teachers must be consistent with the rights they are teaching about. It is important to build a culture in which human rights are respected for all members of the school community. Human rights need to be incorporated into all school policies through negotiation and involvement of all members of the school community, in order that children and teachers are aware of what their rights, and consequent responsibilities, are and how to exercise them.

Many forms of discrimination exist in every society. Children will bring into the school attitudes, beliefs and behaviours they have learned from their families and communities, some of which may include negative attitudes towards some groups of children – for example, assumptions as to the superiority of boys, contempt for lower class or poor children, hatred of different religions, ethnic groups or cultures, or belief in the stupidity of children with disabilities. Not only do these attitudes and the behaviours that accompany them violate the rights of many children, they also impede their education. Children who are systematically discouraged, marginalized and reviled lose confidence and self-esteem, which in turn impacts on their motivation and ability to learn. Schools need to take a proactive role in promoting a culture of inclusion and respect for all children, through both the formal curriculum and the way the school is run.

## Respecting identity

### Language of instruction

In many countries, there is a significant proportion of children for whom the language of instruction is not their mother tongue, imposing a major obstacle to learning. In the Lao People's Democratic Republic, for example, which is ethnically and linguistically diverse, there is a high drop-out rate at primary level and almost all children in secondary school are those with Lao as a first language.[98] There is no simple solution to the challenge of providing education in countries where there are multiple languages spoken. There is no explicit obligation on States to ensure that all children can be taught in their first language, and States are entitled to determine the languages of instruction. In many countries, policies of unilingualism are adopted as a strategy towards integration and nation building, although others do recognize the existence and significance of linguistic diversity and acknowledge an official multilingual approach. This may be addressed through schools providing different languages of instruction. However, there is an implication that States should facilitate the use of a child's first language especially in the earliest years of education. Research has shown that "learners learn best in their mother tongue as a prelude to and complement of bilingual education approaches."[99]

The use of children's mother tongue in school is pedagogically sound. It encourages community mobilization and social development, overcomes exclusion and marginalization, and provides for a political voice. It also increases economic opportunity and mobility.[100] Research demonstrates the importance of building a strong educational foundation in a child's first language if she or he is to be successful in the second and additional languages. Furthermore, it indicates that States can realize a cost saving through a reduction in the numbers of students who repeat grades when children are educated in their mother tongue and in bilingual schooling systems.[101] Schools can teach in the local languages of children by recruiting native speakers. In Peru, for example, an initiative to apply bilingual education in multigrade classes for local language speakers has contributed to a 50 per cent increase in writing and communications skills among students.[102] The Convention on the Rights of Persons with Disabilities also stresses the right of children who are blind or deaf to be taught in the "most appropriate languages and modes and means of communication for the individual, and in environments which maximize academic and social development."[103]

## Multilingualism

UNESCO has developed a position paper on multilingualism that supports:

- Mother tongue instruction as a means of improving educational quality by building on the knowledge and experience of the learners and teachers.

- Bilingual and/or multilingual education as a means of promoting social and gender equality and a key element of linguistically diverse societies.

- Language learning as an essential part of intercultural education to encourage understanding between different groups and respect for fundamental rights.

Source: United Nations Educational, Scientific and Cultural Organization, 'Education in a Multilingual World', Education Position Paper, UNESCO, Paris, 2003, p. 30.

## Inclusion of indigenous children

Child-friendly schools have been promoted since 2000 in two states in Mexico characterized by high marginalization and a large indigenous population. Child-friendly schools promote high quality education for indigenous boys and girls in a 'friendly' school environment for learning. School plays a critical role in generating positive changes in the participation of the children, teachers and parents, and in achieving sustainable development in the context of indigenous people's own culture. Child-friendly schools seek to improve learning through intercultural and bilingual teaching; foster active participation by students, families and the community; and promote civic education based on democratic values, respect for diversity and promotion of equity, cooperation and participation. They also work towards a healthy, clean and friendly school environment.

A parallel initiative in community participative learning promotes civic education and activities through which families and communities learn about the rights of children in a culturally appropriate and respectful manner and are encouraged to participate in the organization of community life around the school. In addition, efforts under the 'All Children in School' initiative seek to strengthen efforts to ensure basic education of high quality for all boys and girls. Evaluation shows better school results, better trained and more motivated teachers, improvement of school environments (including toilets and water facilities), increased community participation and integration in education, and a heightened sense of indigenous identity, contributing to higher self-esteem.

**Source:** Mexico Country Office, internal United Nations Children's Fund document.

### Religious and cultural rights

There is no single approach to respecting religious and cultural rights in education systems. Separate schooling systems for different religions or languages can serve to discriminate against and marginalize groups of children if the schools are afforded inequitable funding and status. They can also serve to exclude and marginalize children from educational and employment opportunities. Conversely, the imposition of a uniform schooling system that takes no account of minority cultures and religions can serve to oppress and undermine children from those communities and contribute to educational failure and high drop-out rates.

There are, however, core obligations for States under the Convention on the Rights of the Child, the International Covenant on Economic, Social and Cultural Rights and the Convention against Discrimination in Education:

- Respect must be afforded to the freedom of parents and guardians to have the religious and moral education of their children in conformity with their convictions.
- Education in the general history of religion and ethics is permitted if it is given in an unbiased and objective way that is respectful of freedoms of opinion, conscience and expression. However, parents must be provided with the possibility of alternative education that accommodates their wishes.
- Indigenous children or those belonging to a minority shall not be denied the right to enjoy their own culture, to profess and practise their own religion, or to use their own language.
- Members of national minorities are entitled to develop their own educational activities, provided so doing does not serve to exclude them from the culture and language of the wider community, and that the standard of education is not lower than the general standard provided for others.
- Parents and guardians can choose other than public education for their children as long as the schools comply with the aims of education elaborated in article 29 of the Convention on the Rights of the Child and minimum standards established by the government, including, for example, a prohibition on physical and humiliating punishments. Inspection and regulation systems need to be in place to ensure compliance with these standards.
- Respect for the liberty of parents and guardians must not be allowed to lead to extreme disparities of educational opportunity between different groups in society. [104]

Intercultural education based on the principles of a rights-based approach can provide a framework for action in countries with indigenous and immigrant cultures different from that of the majority.[105]

## Policies to ensure children's participation

In addition to an underpinning legal framework, States need to introduce mechanisms for children's participation at all levels in the education system. Action might include:

- Consultative systems for children to contribute to the development of education policy at national and regional levels.
- Guidance and training for schools on establishing schools councils, involving children in the development of school policies, and developing and sustaining democratic school environments.
- Introduction of human and children's rights, including rights to participation, both in pre- and in-service training of teachers.
- Involvement of children as both researchers and respondents in systems for monitoring and evaluating education systems.

## "The school does better when the pupils govern"

Governments, non-governmental organizations and other partners, teachers, parents and students themselves seek schools in which children learn, schools that are safe, clean, enriching, fair, gender-sensitive, inclusive, child-centred and community-based. Children's governments have been successful in transforming schools into exactly these things, and it is mainly through the active participation of the students that these changes have been possible. While children are often asked in school to sit down, quiet down and settle down, a children's government encourages children to stand up, speak up and take action.

### What is a children's government?

A children's government is a tool to promote child participation, to further quality education, and to improve school and community life. With discrete guidance from adults, and through role play, the students organize themselves into ministries, elect ministers, make decisions, take actions and hold themselves (and the adults) accountable for fulfilling their responsibilities. Through their participation in children's government, children learn about citizenship rights and responsibilities, and problem-solving and communication skills, and have the chance to experience an environment of team spirit and one in which girls and boys are treated equally. Children's governments are allowing children not only to learn about democracy and peace, social justice and gender equality, but also to exercise their freedom of expression (and self-discipline) and to become true decision makers. One of the countries where this tool is being used is Mali.

Children can also play a key role in advocating for their education rights. For example, national-level demonstrations of secondary students in Chile prompted the Government to place the issue of the quality of education at the top of its agenda.[106] When creating opportunities for children to participate, it is also necessary to take appropriate measures to ensure they are protected from manipulation, violence, abuse or exploitation and that the process takes account of their evolving capacities and is designed to promote their best interests (*see Appendix VI, page 131*).

### How does a children's government work?

While adults provide guidance to the children on how to form a government and how to engage in activities and achieve certain goals, children elect ministers and delegates, diagnose the needs of the school, draw up action plans, take action, and then reflect on their experience. Ministers and delegates of a children's government are not elected according to prior experience but rather according to their personal qualities, such as kindness and good communication and organization skills. An equal number of girls and boys must be elected. Each student elected holds her or his term for one year. The number of ministers depends on the problems and needs identified by the students at the beginning of each school year.

Children's governments work to improve many different aspects of school and community life, such as education, health, protection, water and AIDS awareness. Activities include tutoring, initiating dialogue with teachers, holding awareness-raising campaigns, improving the school's physical environment and practising good hygiene. These activities and other actions are initiated by children but can involve various members of the community, such as parents and religious leaders. Thus, children's talents are allowed to flourish through planning and action.

**Source:** Traoré, Fousséni, 'Quand les élèves gouvernent, l'école va mieux', *Le Républicain*, 16 March 2004, p. 1.

## Protecting integrity

While legislation to bring an end to violence in schools is a necessary prerequisite, it is not sufficient to achieve violence-free schools. In some countries that have introduced laws prohibiting physical punishment in schools, the practice continues to be widespread.[107] Parents often actively encourage teachers to use such punishment. Policies and guidance are therefore necessary to support the implementation of legislation prohibiting physical punishment in all educational settings, including:[108]

## A model for promoting non-violence in school

In one province of Argentina, school mediation training has been given to all teachers since 1998. The aim is to raise awareness of the prevalence of violence and its associated attitudes and teach them alternative conflict resolution methods, such as negotiation and mediation. A mediation programme based on this learning has been extended to all schools. The premise underpinning the programme is that friction and conflict always exist in institutions, but it is possible to identify non-violent strategies for addressing this.

One of the basic techniques used for the peaceful management of conflict is to understand other people's feelings, decipher their culture and comprehend their differences without viewing them as failings. A central dimension in the approach is to gain an awareness of other people's attitudes and how these affect behaviour. This can be done by the creation of a forum for sharing day-to-day problems and analysing one's own attitudes without being judged. The key tools of negotiation and mediation are dialogue and listening. In addition, the importance of promoting non-violence can be applied throughout the curriculum, for example:

- **Geography** – conflicts between neighbouring countries.
- **Literature** – analysis of literary works and the discussion this stimulates.
- **Physical education** – by elaborating the rules of the game.
- **Mathematics** – by analysing the various ways of solving a problem.

- **Information for children** about their rights to protection from all forms of violence and their consequent responsibilities not to use violence against others, including teachers.
- **Peace education** that introduces ideas of non-violent conflict resolution and teaches children such skills as mediation, listening and negotiation as tools for dealing with conflict.
- **Training for teachers** on the rights of children, the counterproductive impact of physical punishment on children's education, the harm that it can cause and strategies for promoting classroom discipline through non-violent methods.

### A successful application of the programme

A conflict arose between final-year pupils at a secondary school over where to hold the end-of-year party. All attempts to negotiate had failed, and the situation was so embittered that the class was on the verge of splitting into two camps: one wanting to hold the party in a club, the other preferring another venue. Each group was determined to boycott the event if it did not have its way. A one-hour lesson was turned into a mediation session led by a teacher who transformed the conflict into a pedagogic exercise. He began by explaining the basic rules of mediation, such as refraining from verbally attacking or interrupting speakers. After each group had stated its position, the work consisted in detecting their interests and perceptions: Group A thought that group B was merely trying to impose its will on the group as a whole, whereas group B claimed that the others had a vested interest in holding the party in a particular place. Group B felt it was 'always' up to them to make decisions in the class due to the passivity of group A. The teacher described the experiment in the following terms: "Our work consisted in using communication techniques so that the two parties would listen to each other, so that they could comment on their own respective perceptions in order to define and become aware of their common and conflicting interests. The interests were written up on the board and served as a basis for brainstorming ideas. When time had run out, each group appointed a representative to reach an agreement. In the end they agreed to hold the party in a third place where they would all attend." Mediation was used in this case as a learning process that allowed the two groups to modify their interpretation of the other group's intentions, which led to an improvement in relations in the class.

**Source:** de Porfirio, Irma Zalazar, Teresita Noemi Codutti and Daniel F. Martinez Zampa, 'Experiments in conflict management and school mediation', in *Best Practices of Non-Violent Conflict Resolution in and out-of-school: Some examples*, United Nations Educational, Scientific and Cultural Organization, Paris, 2002, pp. 11–14.

- **A requirement for schools to introduce school behaviour policies** that both promote and support strategies for non-violent conflict resolution, do not tolerate adults or children bullying or perpetrating acts of violence against other students, and actively engage children in their development.
- **Sensitization programmes with parents** to enable them to understand why physical punishment should not be used, children's right to protection from violence and the detrimental impact of violence on children's learning.
- **Safe and accessible complaints mechanisms** to enable children to challenge violations of their rights.
- **Media campaigns** to promote awareness of children's right to protection from violence.

UNESCO has produced a range of tools for peace education and promoting non-violence in schools. At the International Forum for Education on Non-Violence in 1996, guidelines for a Plan of Action were developed. These guidelines provide an important framework for building conflict resolution.[109] In addition, *The World Report on Violence Against Children* has developed detailed recommendations for action in addressing violence in schools.[110] These resources need to be available to teachers (*see Bibliography, page 102*).

© UNICEF/ HQ06-2426/Susan Markisz

# THE ROLE OF OTHER DUTY BEARERS

States cannot fulfil their obligations with regard to rights-based education without the active support and engagement of many other actors, including parents, extended family members, unions, teachers, religious communities, civil society organizations and local politicians. Human rights are not simply legal entitlements that can be realized through the enactment of legislation and policy. They are standards and principles that directly affect the day-to-day relationships between individuals in their communities. The creation of a sustainable and rights-respecting education for all children requires that the concept of education is understood and owned by parents, families and all members of the community. Education is not an isolated activity. The actions, attitudes and behaviours of all members of communities affect the realization or denial of rights in education.

From the state level down to the individual parent lie differing levels of obligation for fulfilling the right to education, but it is essential that clear and appropriate lines of accountability are drawn. For example, parents cannot fulfil their obligations to ensure that their child is prepared for and attends school on a regular basis unless the government has provided the schools and the economic environment to support that attendance. Recognition also needs to be given to the fact that every adult has rights as well as responsibilities. Parents, for example, have responsibilities to ensure their children's access to education, but they also have a right to education. Teachers are entitled to respect, remuneration and appropriate training and support, and they cannot fulfil their obligations to children unless these rights are realized. As discussed in Chapter 1, there is a close interrelationship between rights and responsibilities. Respect for human rights is not contingent on the exercise of responsibilities, but rights can only be realized if those responsibilities are taken seriously.

It also needs to be acknowledged that some of the actors involved in children's lives can serve as barriers to the right to education. A necessary dimension of a rights-based approach is to work with these actors to overcome the concerns that impede access to education. It is important to enlist the knowledge, skills and energies of all those involved. Children's opportunities to attend school will be influenced by parental recognition of their right to an education, the extent to which the school welcomes their attendance, and freedom from the necessity to work. Children's commitment to education will be influenced by the regard in which it is held in their community, by the relevance and the quality of the education they receive and by the respect with which they are treated in the school. Children's achievements in education will be influenced by the degree of support they receive at home, the quality of teachers, the teaching methods employed, the extent to which they are engaged as actors in the educational process, the availability of the necessary teaching aids and resources, and a willingness to offer the necessary flexibility to facilitate their regular attendance. All these factors can be supported through government action. But they rely, for their implementation, on the mobilization of all members of the community.

This chapter discusses the role of parents and other caregivers, communities, teachers, civil society organizations and the international community.

## PARENTS AND OTHER CAREGIVERS

Parents and other caregivers have key responsibilities in supporting and facilitating children's access to education. In many societies, particularly those with large populations of orphans, it is members of the extended family who are caring for children. In these circumstances, they have obligations in respect of those children's rights. Parents and other caregivers provide the initial stages for learning in the life of a child. They are also vital partners in their children's continuing education; without parents' engagement, children's chances of gaining access and sustaining a commitment to education are significantly diminished.

### Parental responsibilities

The contribution of parents can include:

- Providing an environment in the early years that ensures the child's preparedness to start school.

- Supporting and recognizing the right to education and the value of education for all their children.
- Ensuring that children are not overburdened with domestic and other work to the detriment of their schooling. Parents need to create space and time in children's lives to enable them to attend school and do their homework.
- Ensuring that children are prepared for school and able to arrive, ready and on time, when school is in session.
- Getting involved in the school and supporting its work – through participation in fund-raising, meetings with teachers, committees, consultations, governing bodies, etc.
- Showing encouragement and support for their child's work and, where possible, helping with homework.
- Advocating for children's right to education – holding schools and education authorities to account in fulfilling their obligations to children, monitoring progress and challenging rights violations.
- Ensuring, to the extent possible, that their children are healthy and well nourished so they are able to learn.
- Ensuring that local traditions and customs, such as child marriage, do not prevent their children from going to school.

An example of parents' advocacy comes from Jordan, where a community meeting of mothers concerned about the lack of secondary education for their daughters led to the preparation of a petition and a meeting with the director of the education ministry. The outcome was the establishment of three fully equipped girls' secondary classes within six months.[111]

## Provision of education for parents

Where parents, particularly mothers, have not been to school, the likelihood of their children realizing their right to education is significantly diminished.[112] A vital dimension in a rights-based approach to education is the provision of adult education, through such facilities as community learning centres, to build the capacity of parents.[113] Local authorities, together with national governments, have the primary responsibility for creating such opportunities to fulfil the rights of parents who were denied access to education in their own childhoods. Without this investment, there is a risk that the right to education will be denied across generations.

Parenting education programmes also need to acknowledge the different support and information required by parents at different stages of their children's lives. It is often assumed that parenting support is only required for preschool children. In practice, the demands of parenting change, and parents can benefit from advice and information on the evolving capacities of children throughout childhood. If parents acquire skills in reading and writing, they can more fully communicate with their children, help them with their schoolwork and better understand what their children are doing at school. For parents of children with serious hearing impairments, learning to sign is essential if they are to communicate with their child. With education, parents will acquire greater capacity to support their children's education from birth, greater understanding of their children's needs and more confidence in collaborating with schools to help improve the quality of education provided. The promotion of equal gender practices is an essential part of all parenting education programmes.

### Parents as partners

Many parents lack the skills, knowledge and resources to interact effectively with teachers and school authorities, while on the part of schools there is often a lack of commitment to reach out to parents. Yet, investment in parents may be as important in the education of a child as the direct learning in school. Schools need to organize regular meetings of parents to share with them the goals of the school, the curriculum that is being taught and updates on the child's progress to enable them to better understand the child's education. Such contact enlists parents as partners in the educational process. Schools can also encourage parents to assist in the classroom, help out in the wider school environment and become members of school boards. Their involvement not only leads to the contribution of practical skills and energy but also increases the sense of ownership of the school, and with it a commitment to children's effective education.

Local groups, such as parents' associations or mothers' clubs, are vital in supporting children's education. Through cooperative organizing, parents can become effective advocates for improved standards and provision. They can work to support the school, monitor children's progress and hold the school to account on its achievements. Such clubs and associations can also play an important role in capacity-building because they create opportunities to develop skills in organizing committees, fund-raising, public speaking and networking.

## COMMUNITIES

Children live not only in families but also in communities, whose values, culture and level of engagement have a significant impact on their day-to-day lives.

Local communities have a key role to play in encouraging environments that are conducive to fulfilling the right to education for every child.

## The community school model

Community schools have been established as a means of providing quality education for children living in small rural hamlets in Egypt, where primary schools were previously non-existent and rural girls were particularly deprived. Modelled after the BRAC experience in Bangladesh, the schools are located in the communities themselves, and hidden costs – from uniforms to school bags – are removed. Local ownership is a key feature, with communities donating space, ensuring that children come to class and managing the schools through a local education committee established in each hamlet. Young women with intermediate degrees are recruited locally and trained as facilitators to provide quality education through interactive techniques. And the content of education is made relevant to local needs and interests, including health, environment, agriculture and local history. Graduates from community schools are eligible for exams in government schools at the end of grades 3 and 6.

The project is serving as a catalyst for development, bringing changes in gender roles and expectations for the girl students as well as for the women facilitators. Lessons from the quality components of the community school model are being brought into the mainstream education system, and the model is being replicated through the establishment of additional girl-friendly schools.

**Source:** United Nations Children's Fund, 'Examples from the Field: UNICEF and Girls' Education in Rural Areas', paper prepared by UNICEF for the ECOSOC Ministerial Roundtable on Primary Education and Girls' Education in Rural Areas, 30 April 2003, p. 2.

## Promoting local awareness

In collaboration with partners in the community, local authorities, including traditional leaders, have the responsibility of promoting awareness of the value of education among local communities and enlisting their support for local schools and the right of all children to education. Work needs to be undertaken with parents and the wider family, as well as religious and other community groups, to help them recognize the benefits of education. Parents may need help in decreasing the domestic workload in order to release children to attend school, for example, through improved access to water or provision of day care for younger children so that girls are relieved of childcare responsibilities. Establishing partnerships with organizations of marginalized and vulnerable people, including children, to develop and lead such programmes is a key strategy for challenging prejudices and stereotypes.

## Analysing local barriers

In any locality, it will be necessary for local authorities – and when appropriate, traditional leaders – to undertake in partnership with community members an analysis of where the barriers to education lie, in which communities and in relation to which children. Action can then be taken to address the specific barriers that arise. This might include:

- Raising awareness on the right to education.
- Promoting the value of education for both girls' and boys' future opportunities.
- Ensuring sensitization as to the nature of disability and the capacity of children with disabilities to benefit from education.
- Stressing the importance of play as part of children's learning and development.
- Providing information about available stipends, cash transfers or food-for-education programmes.
- Addressing parental concerns, such as violence when travelling to school.
- Adapting school timetables to accommodate domestic labour commitments.
- Highlighting the role parents can play in supporting and strengthening their children's learning, including the importance of active engagement in the life of the school and the ways in which parents and communities can contribute.
- Listening to children and engaging them as active participants in their own learning.
- Promoting respect for children as learners and ending all forms of violence in schools.

## Providing accurate information on the preschool and school-aged population

Information at the local level on the preschool and school-aged population is needed to determine that the availability of places, trained teachers and educational resources is consistent with the size of that population. The process of mapping can be undertaken in partnership with local non-governmental organizations, traditional leaders, community members, religious organizations or parent groups. Efforts need to be made to include the less visible children, such as those with disabilities and children of migrant and domestic workers. As noted in the previous chapter, birth registration is an important factor in building up accurate records of child populations.

## Supporting schools

Local community members can generate critical advocacy for education and raise resources to improve school facilities. They can contribute financial support, organize fund-raising activities, join school governing bodies, support community-based curricula activities, contribute to 'working parties' to maintain the school environment, campaign for improved funding, help adapt school buildings so they are more accessible for children with disabilities and encourage the elimination of child labour in their communities. The active involvement of the local community raises the status of the school and lends support to a perception that education is important and must be valued and protected for all children. However, it needs to be recognized that communities are not homogeneous. Efforts to promote community involvement should include poor and marginalized households, and particular efforts may be required to achieve that goal.

# TEACHERS

While the wider educational infrastructure is vital, it is teachers who have the most impact on the day-to-day experience of children in school. A quality education, in which children want to take part, is dependent on the commitment, enthusiasm, creativity and skill of teachers. It is their task to translate national policies into practical action in each school and to ensure that they embrace a culture that is inclusive and respectful of every child. In order for this to happen, as discussed earlier, teachers' rights must also be fully acknowledged and respected.[114]

## Head teachers

While governments have responsibility for setting the terms and conditions of teachers' work and for promoting a culture of respect for their work, much can be done at the local level to uphold the rights of teachers. Head teachers have responsibilities for advancing teachers' rights, providing appropriate support, addressing concerns, involving teachers in decision-making in the school and promoting respect for their work in the local community. They also need to help teachers understand their roles and responsibilities and monitor their behaviour. It is important that teachers feel respected and valued, as this will enhance their capacity and willingness to respect the rights of children.

## The school under the mango tree

The Sementinha, or school under the mango tree, was first established for 4- to 6-year-olds in a city in Brazil in response to the many young children not attending school. The methodology is based on the ideas of circle and play. Each day starts with the children sitting in a circle and being asked, "What shall we study today?" Participation is a fundamental principle and all children, regardless of age, have a right to contribute. Initially, they were unable to express themselves, but with encouragement from the teachers, they gradually built up confidence and began to put forward opinions. All group questions are resolved in a circle, which is a space for talking, listening, arguing, reflecting and reaching consensus. In this way, children do not feel excluded if their ideas are rejected. The children also have a role in assessing the activities. This is done through verbal discussion, as well as drawing, singing, creating stories and writing poems. The children's feedback is taken seriously by the teachers and informs future activities. The teachers also meet in a circle before school begins to discuss their plans, and again at the end of the day to review the activities that have taken place.

The school is inextricably linked with the local community. The project does not rely on a building to provide a quality education, and teaching can take place in the neighbourhood, the streets, a church hall or someone's house. The teachers and children are constantly moving around the community, so parents and others can actually see their children learning. Initially, many parents objected to the methodology of the school. They felt that education could only take place in a building with paper and pencils. The project addressed this by involving parents in the circles and exploring with them the way the school worked. Parents began to notice differences in their children, who became more stimulated and developed than children at other schools. Children also use the 'circle time' methods to try to resolve family conflicts at home.

The model offers a good start in early childhood and stimulates parents to be involved in their children's education. It has been adapted to work in rural, small-town and city environments, and has been replicated in 13 towns, involving 3,300 children and 165 teachers.

**Source:** Guerra, Rosangela, 'The School under the Mango Tree: Mighty children grow from little seeds', an interview with Tião Rocha in *Early Childhood Matters*, no. 103, Bernard van Leer Foundation, November 2004, pp. 21–26.

## Duties of teachers

### Introducing practical measures for inclusion

Schools have a key role to play in translating policies of inclusion into the day-to-day life of education. All children need to feel welcome and confident of equal treatment in the school. Schools need to promote an atmosphere of respect for all children. They should instigate a culture that ensures that no bias is tolerated that favours or discriminates against any learner or group of learners – whether in respect of admission procedures, treatment in the classroom, opportunities for learning, access to examinations, opportunities to participate in particular activities, such as music or drama, or marking of work. Children should never be stereotyped or insulted on the basis of who or what they are. Teachers need to take active measures to involve girls on an equal basis with boys. Schools need to develop policies setting out the principles of non-discrimination and ensure that all teachers, parents and children are aware of the policy and know how to make a complaint if it is breached. Children and parents should be involved in the development of the policy as this will strengthen ownership and understanding. The process of developing the policy is also an opportunity to address the issues, learn why they are important, and develop skills in negotiation, listening and understanding different points of view and experiences.

### Promoting a respectful environment

Schools need to develop policies to promote an environment of respect throughout the school. These policies should be developed through collaboration with all stakeholders, including children. For example, policy and guidance can be provided on: how to promote a non-violent approach to conflict resolution both between teachers and children and among children themselves; how to promote children's active participation in school decision-making processes; and how to develop school codes of behaviour that govern the relationships between all members of the school community and contribute to educational processes. These guidelines can be adapted and developed by individual schools, involving children, parents and teachers, all of whom need to feel ownership of the subsequent policies.

### Accommodating differing needs

Inclusion necessitates action to accommodate children's differing needs. It may be necessary, for example, to ensure that some classes are held on ground floors to accommodate wheelchair users. Schools can pilot models of education that allow more flexible participation in the classroom, take classes to where children are located or organize different hours of teaching. Starting times could be staggered, with different groups of children arriving at different times to enable children to learn in flexible groups that take account of external demands on their time, such as agricultural work or domestic labour, although it is vital not to reduce the often already limited learning time available to them. Some schools in Bangladesh have a flexible schedule that runs for limited hours, six days a week, with the times set by local parents and the school calendar adapted to accommodate local considerations, such as harvests.[115] Depending on their age, children need regular breaks to help them rest and learn effectively, particularly those children who come to school having already undertaken paid work or domestic chores. Children can work on a modular basis or in groups where they learn together in accordance with the hours they can attend, and also in tutoring initiatives that are often provided in complementary or after-school programmes.

## Encouraging local engagement

Child-friendly schools need to be responsive to the local context. Within a framework of core standards and principles, individual schools should be able to adapt to the needs of the local community and provide a relevant curriculum that takes account of local concerns and priorities. For example, some schools have made children's participation in managing the environment of the school and local community integral to the basic concept of the school as a community-based centre for democratic learning.[116]

## Engaging children as partners

Schools need to promote environments in which children are engaged as active participants at all levels:[117] as peer educators and mentors for younger children; in setting up and running school councils that act as a forum for addressing children's concerns; in helping develop school policy, including behaviour codes and discipline; in advising on such issues as playground design, and location and design of latrines; in contributing to the curriculum; in providing feedback and evaluation on the curriculum and teaching methods; as mediators helping resolve conflicts; and in participating on school governing bodies. One approach to creating a participatory environment is to employ the use of 'circle time', a process whereby children come together each day in a circle to discuss issues of concern to them, identify problems and explore solutions (*see 'The school under the mango tree', page 94*). Children can also be involved in establishing the indicators used to monitor how well a school is respecting the rights of all its members, and they can take part in a process of regular evaluation of compliance with those indicators. They can then share in the responsibility of developing strategies for improving practice. In all these strategies, efforts need to be made to ensure equal opportunities for participation by all children.

**Balancing rights and responsibilities**

Teaching children about their rights involves understanding the reciprocal responsibilities these imply. While a child has a right to be listened to and have her or his views given due weight, she or he has a corresponding responsibility to listen to the views of others. This learning can only take place through the experience of how children are treated in the school and the culture of mutual respect it promotes. One example is accommodating children who live far away or have domestic or other work commitments to complete before school. Instead of punishing children who continually arrive late on the basis that it will serve as an incentive to arrive earlier, it would be valuable to meet with children to discuss modifying the timetable, explore changing the starting time or organizing a flexible starting time.

# CIVIL SOCIETY ORGANIZATIONS

In most countries throughout the world, international, national and local civil society organizations play a central role in the realization of rights, whether as service providers or as advocates challenging duty bearers to fulfil their obligations. They are often the source of considerable expertise, not only on where gaps in provision exist in local communities but also on the strategies needed to address those gaps. Building partnerships with these organizations is thus of considerable importance. The private sector is also playing an increasingly important role in the provision of basic services, including education, and needs to comply with its corresponding obligations as a duty bearer. It can therefore be a significant partner in many countries.

## Collaborating in the provision of education

Local or district authorities, including traditional leaders, need to share perspectives and expertise with non-governmental education providers on the needs of children out of school and how to most effectively provide for their education, and to explore strategies for smoother transitions between the non-government and government sectors. This could involve piloting different approaches for promoting educational opportunities for marginalized children. It is invaluable to consult with children in non-government schools because they are an important source of information on why these schools work for them and the changes needed in government schools to accommodate the reality of their lives. Positive factors for children in non-government schools relate to the more informal and creative aspects of the curriculum and the quality of relationships they have with the teachers. The downside, however, is the lack of opportunity for accreditation and the possible sense of social exclusion associated with attending schools that may be stigmatized by low status and marginalization.[118] Efforts need to be made to overcome these problems and build on the strengths associated with both government and non-government schools if the equal right of these children to an education is to be made a reality. Initiatives to pilot models of inclusion can also be undertaken at the local level in partnership with organizations of people with disabilities, parents and local non-governmental and community organizations.

## Mobilizing and capacity-building

Civil society organizations have often been at the forefront of mobilizing society to claim rights. Such organizations engage with the poorest, most marginalized and vulnerable in a community and help develop their capacities and assist in identifying spaces and entry points whereby such groups can engage with duty bearers to realize rights. In a way, such organizations have a demand-supply role. On the demand side, this role has been played through advocacy, lobbying and ensuring accountability and transparency of duty bearers, for example, monitoring whether governmental policies and programmes have been effectively implemented. It can also involve helping guarantee the continuation of successful programmes when there are changes of government or administration. On the supply side, this has been undertaken by capacity-building of:

- **Communities, parents and traditional leaders** – through training, awareness and sensitization to enable communities to participate in, for instance, social auditing and monitoring exercises of government services.
- **Governments** – by training and sensitization of public officials.

Through the provision of alternative models of social relations that are often empowering and participatory, and involve the most vulnerable in achieving outcomes, civil society organizations can be credited with helping to democratize the processes of social change to claim rights.

# CHAPTER 4

# THE INTERNATIONAL COMMUNITY

The international community can be a major participant in the realization of the right to education as it provides support to build the capacity of both governments and individuals. The Dakar Framework for Action expressly introduces a role for the international community, for example, in the allocation of a larger share of resources to support primary and other forms of basic education, and in ensuring that education strategies complement other strategies for poverty elimination, such as the United Nations Development Assistance Framework (UNDAF) and poverty reduction strategy papers. The recent Paris Declaration on Aid Effectiveness also moves development partners towards such rights-based approaches in terms of, for example, capacity-building and accountability.[119] This role has been further affirmed in the Organisation for Economic Co-operation and Development/Development Co-operation Directorate Report 'Integrating Human Rights in Development', which calls on development partners to:

- Deepen their institutionalization of human rights considerations, looking at their systems, procedures and staff incentives and allocating adequate resources to better translate their policies into practice.
- Support the strengthening of national ownership of human rights in the context of development partnerships, particularly around poverty reduction strategies.
- Push for the integration of human rights into thinking and practice around new aid effectiveness processes and instruments and modalities of aid delivery.[120]

## Strategies for promoting rights-based education

Development partners can utilize a range of strategies in their programming for rights-based education, including:

- **Providing technical expertise and building capacity** to help States meet their international human rights commitments.
- **Facilitating stakeholders' capacity to claim their rights** – this will involve training and support on human rights to enhance their capacity to advocate for and claim their rights, and the creation of opportunities for them to do so.
- **Holding States to account** – partners with a commitment to the human rights of children have obligations to hold States to account on the commitments they have made in ratifying international human rights treaties.

- **Building strategic partnerships to strengthen efficiency** – agencies need to collaborate effectively to ensure the greatest possible efficiency and effectiveness in programming and development cooperation at both the global and national levels. The UN Reform process, as well as the Rome Declaration on Harmonisation and Simplification spearheaded by the Organisation for Economic Co-operation and Development/Development Co-operation Directorate, seeks to achieve this objective. The non-governmental sector also needs to collaborate with partners to maximize effectiveness.
- **Building systemic change** – in the long run, the most disadvantaged are clearly best served by a non-discriminating and fully inclusive education system. Overall, therefore, investment needs to be made in programmes that have the potential to achieve large-scale systemic change. Until such reforms have been introduced, it remains essential to provide support to the most vulnerable groups, including through compensatory and positive discrimination programmes. Targeted interventions will only cease to be necessary when national standards are set, adhered to and monitored by communities.[121]
- **Support collection and analysis of data** from a national, regional and international perspective to facilitate informed policymaking. This will also help identify promising programmes or practices, analyse the conditions under which those best practices can be adopted by countries facing similar challenges and allow for cross-country comparisons of progress.

## Issues to address in promoting rights-based education

Some additional challenges posed by a rights-based approach to the way in which funding is provided need to be addressed. These include time scales, outcomes and indicators, and sector-wide approaches.

### Time scales

Rights-based approaches that involve changing the culture of education systems towards greater respect for children as active participants in the education process take time. It is not always possible to achieve these objectives in tight two- to three-year time frames. Donors need to be sensitive to the complexity of the changes needed, although governments and international agencies clearly still need to be accountable to donors for the funds they receive.

## Outcomes and indicators

Donors need to recognize the importance of indicators beyond the traditional data collection on enrolment, attendance and attainment, for example, gathering data relating to non-violence, inclusion and participation.

## Sector-wide approaches

Rights-based education is consistent with the principles of sector-wide approaches *(see pages 43–44)*, which provide comprehensive and coherent strategies encompassing all aspects of education. Discrete projects funded by individual donors can serve to fragment such an approach and introduce inconsistency in terms of objectives, goals, monitoring and reporting. The Paris Declaration emphasizes the need for donors to reform policies to encourage "collaborative behaviour and progressive alignment with partner countries' priorities, systems and procedures."[122] The challenge is to ensure that those priorities, systems and procedures are sufficiently widely drawn to encompass the full range of policies necessary to ensure the right to education.

As this chapter has demonstrated, the role of other duty bearers in fulfilling children's right to education and rights within education underlines the intrinsic link of rights-based approaches to just and equitable socioeconomic development.

In conclusion, education rights cannot be realized without the fulfilment of other rights, without the active engagement of all social actors in taking up their responsibilities and without a vision of social change. This framework for the realization of children's right to education and rights within education is one step forward in guiding action towards this goal. It is anticipated that it will be used by governments, UN agencies, non-governmental organizations and donors in their ongoing work to achieve education for all.

# SELECTED BIBLIOGRAPHY

Annan, Kofi, 'In Larger Freedom: Towards development, security and human rights for all', Report of the Secretary-General, United Nations General Assembly Fifty-ninth Session, March 2005.

Booth, Tony, and Mel Ainslow, *Index for Inclusion: Developing learning and participation in schools*, Centre for Studies on Inclusive Education, Bristol, 2000.

Bush, Kenneth D., and Diana Saltarelli, eds., *The Two Faces of Education in Ethnic Conflict: Towards a peacebuilding education for children,* UNICEF Innocenti Research Centre, Florence, 2000.

CARE Human Rights Initiative, 'Basic Introduction to Human Rights and Rights-Based Programming: Facilitators' guidebook', Care International, London, 2004, <www.reliefweb.int/rw/rwt.nsf/db900SID/NVEA-5ULK9G/$File/care-hrguide.pdf?OpenElement>, accessed 29 June 2007.

Crisp, Jeff, Christopher Talbot and Daiana B. Cipollone, eds., *Learning for a Future: Refugee education in developing countries*, United Nations Refugee Agency, Geneva, 2001.

Dahlberg, Gunilla, Peter Moss and Alan Pence, *Beyond Quality in Early Childhood Education and Care,* Routledge/Falmer, London and New York, 1999.

Delors, Jacques, *Learning: The treasure within*, Report to UNESCO of the International Commission on Education for the Twenty-first Century, UNESCO Publishing, Paris, 1996.

Frankovits, André, 'Mainstreaming Human Rights: The human rights-based approach and the United Nations system', desk study prepared for UNESCO, 2005.

Fountain, Susan, *It's Only Right! A practical guide to learning about the Convention on the Rights of the Child*, United Nations Children's Fund, New York, 1993.

Furniss, Elaine, *Assessing Learning Achievement,* United Nations Children's Fund, New York, 2003.

Graham-Brown, Sarah, 'The Role of the Curriculum', Chapter 6, *Education Rights and Minorities*, Minority Rights Group, London, 1994.

Grimshaw, Patricia, Katie Holmes and Marilyn Lake, eds., *Women's Rights and Human Rights: International historical perspectives*, Palgrave, London, 2001.

Hammarberg, Thomas, *A School for Children with Rights: The significance of the United Nations Convention on the Rights of the Child for modern education policy*, UNICEF Innocenti Research Centre, Florence, 1998.

Hart, Roger, with Alfhild Petren, 'The right to play', in Alfhild Petren and James Himes, eds., *Children's Rights: Turning principles into practice,* Save the Children Sweden/UNICEF ROSA, Stockholm, 2000.

Hart, Stuart N. et al., eds., *Eliminating Corporal Punishment: The way forward to constructive child discipline*, UNESCO Publishing, Paris, 2005.

Hodgkin, Rachel, and Peter Newell, *Implementation Handbook on the Convention on the Rights of the Child*, United Nations Children's Fund, New York, 2002.

Human Rights Watch, *Failing our Children: Barriers to education,* HRW, New York, 2005.

Inter-Agency Network for Education in Emergencies, 'Minimum Standards for Education in Emergencies, Chronic Crises and Early Reconstruction', INEE/UNESCO, Paris, 2004.

International Center for the Defense and Promotion of the Rights and Potential of All Children, *Crossing Boundaries: Ideas and experiences in dialogue for a new culture of education of children and adults*, Edizioni Junior, Azzano San Paolo, 2006.

Jochnick, Chris, and Pauline Garzon, *Rights-based Approaches to Development,* CARE and Oxfam America, Atlanta, 2002.

Jonsson, Urban, *A Human Rights Approach to Development Programming,* United Nations Children's Fund, New York, 2003.

Kattan, Raja Bentaouet, 'Implementation of Free Basic Education Policy', *Education Working Paper Series No. 7*, World Bank, Washington, D.C., December 2006.

Kattan, Raja Bentaouet, and Nicholas Burnett, *User Fees in Primary Education*, World Bank, Washington, D.C., 2004.

Kerr, David, *Citizenship Education in Primary Schools*, Institute for Citizenship Studies, London, 1999.

Lansdown, Gerison, *Betrayal of Trust: An overview of Save the Children's findings on children's experience of physical and humiliating punishment, child sexual abuse and violence when in conflict with the law*, Save the Children, Stockholm, 2006.

—, *What's the Difference? Implications of a child-focus in rights-based programming*, discussion paper for Save the Children UK, London, March 2005.

—, *The Evolving Capacities of the Child,* UNICEF Innocenti Research Centre, Florence, 2005.

—, *Promoting Children's Participation in Democratic Decision-Making*, UNICEF Innocenti Research Centre, Florence 2001.

Lawrence, John, *The Right to Education for Persons with Disabilities: Towards inclusion – An EFA flagship paper*, Inclusion International, London, 2004.

Melchiorre, Angela, *At What age? ...are school children employed, married and taken to court*, 2nd ed., Right to Education Project, Lund, 2004.

Nyamu-Musembi, Celestine, and Andrea Cornwall, 'What is the "rights-based approach" all about? Perspectives from international development agencies', *IDS Working Paper 234*, Institute of Development Studies, Brighton, 2004.

Office of the United Nations High Commissioner for Human Rights, *Frequently Asked Questions on a Human Rights-Based Approach to Development Cooperation,* United Nations, New York and Geneva, 2006.

—, *ABC: Teaching human rights, practical activities for primary and secondary schools,* United Nations, New York and Geneva, 2005.

—, *The United Nations Human Rights Treaty System: An introduction to the core human rights treaties and the treaty bodies*, Fact Sheet No. 30, United Nations, Geneva, June 2005, <www.ohchr.org/english/about/publications/docs/fs30.pdf>, accessed 27 June 2007.

—, *Human Rights and Poverty Reduction: A conceptual framework*, United Nations, New York and Geneva, 2004.

Pigozzi, Mary Joy, 'Education in Emergencies and for Reconstruction: A developmental approach', Working Paper Series, Education Section, United Nations Children's Fund, New York, 1999.

Rogoff, Barbara, Eugene Matsuov and Cynthia White, 'Models of Teaching and Learning: Participation in a community of learners', in David R. Olson and Nancy Torrance, eds., *The Handbook of Education and Human Development: New models of learning, teaching and schooling*, Blackwell, Oxford, 1996.

Santos Pais, Marta, 'The Convention on the Rights of the Child', in Office of the High Commissioner for Human Rights, United Nations Institute for Training and Research, and United Nations Staff College Project, *Manual on Human Rights Reporting under Six Major International Human Rights Instruments*, United Nations, Geneva, 1997.

Save the Children, *Child Rights Programming: How to apply rights-based approaches to programming*, 2nd ed., Save the Children Sweden, Stockholm, 2005.

—, *Rights Based Monitoring and Evaluation: A discussion paper,* Save the Children, London, 2003.

—, *Children's rights: equal rights? Diversity, difference and the issue of discrimination*, Save the Children, London, 2000.

Schweisfurth, Michele, Lynn Davies and Clive Harber, eds., *Learning Democracy and Citizenship: International experiences*, Symposium Books, Oxford, 2002.

Smith, Alan, and Tony Vaux, *Education, Conflict and International Development*, Department for International Development, London, 2003.

Symonides, Janusz, ed., *Human Rights: International protection, monitoring, enforcement,* United Nations Educational, Scientific and Cultural Organization, Paris, 2000.

—, *Human Rights: Concept and standards,* United Nations Educational, Scientific and Cultural Organization, Paris and Ashgate, Aldershot, 2000.

—, *Human Rights: New dimensions and challenges,* United Nations Educational, Scientific and Cultural Organization, Paris and Ashgate, Aldershot, 1998.

Symonides, Janusz, and Vladimir Volodine, *A Guide to Human Rights: Institutions, standards, procedures,* United Nations Educational, Scientific and Cultural Organization, Paris, 2001.

—, *Human Rights of Women: A collection of international and regional normative instruments,* United Nations Educational, Scientific and Cultural Organization, Paris, 1999.

Theis, Joachim, *Promoting Rights-Based Approaches: Experiences and ideas from Asia and the Pacific,* Save the Children Sweden, 2004.

Tomaševski, Katarina, *Human Rights Obligations in Education: The 4-A Scheme*, Wolf Legal Publishers, Nijmegen, 2006.

—, *Education Denied: Costs and remedies,* Zed Books, London, 2003.

—, *Racism, Racial Discrimination, Xenophobia and Related Intolerance Relating to Education*, United Nations Educational, Scientific and Cultural Organization, Paris, February 2003.

—, *Human Rights in Education as Prerequisite for Human Rights Education,* Right to Education Primers No. 4, Raoul Wallenberg Institute/Swedish International Development Cooperation Agency, Stockholm, 2001.

Tomaševski, Katarina, and United Nations Educational, Scientific and Cultural Organization Bangkok, *Manual on Rights-Based Education: Global human rights requirements made simple*, UNESCO Bangkok, Bangkok, 2004.

United Nations, 'The Human Rights-Based Approach to Development Cooperation: Towards a common understanding among UN agencies', Report of The Second Interagency Workshop on Implementing a Human Rights-based Approach in the Context of UN Reform, Stamford, May 2003.

United Nations Children's Fund, *The 'Rights' Start to Life: A statistical analysis of birth registration*, UNICEF, New York, 2005.

—, *The State of the World's Children 2004: Girls, education and development*, UNICEF, New York, 2003.

—, 'A League Table of Educational Disadvantage in Rich Nations', *Innocenti Report Card No. 4*, UNICEF Innocenti Research Centre, Florence, November 2002.

—, *Implementation Handbook for the Convention on the Rights of the Child - Fully Revised Edition*, UNICEF, New York, 2002.

—, *The State of the World's Children 1999: Education*, UNICEF, New York, 1998.

—, *Education Rights and Minorities*, UNICEF Innocenti Research Centre, Florence, 1994.

United Nations Children's Fund and Minority Rights Group International, *War: The impact on minority and indigenous children*, Minority Rights Group International, London, 1997.

United Nations Committee on Economic, Social and Cultural Rights, *General Comment No. 16: The equal right of men and women to the enjoyment of all economic, social and cultural rights (article 3),* 2005.

—, *General Comment No. 13: The right to education (article 13)*, 1999.

—, *General Comment No. 11: Plans of action for primary education (article 14)*, 1999.

United Nations Committee on the Elimination of Discrimination against Women, *General Recommendation No. 3: Education and public information programmes,* 1987.

United Nations Committee on the Rights of the Child, *General Comment No. 7: Implementing child rights in early childhood,* 2005.

—, *General Comment No. 4: Adolescent health,* 2003.

—, *General Comment No. 3: HIV/AIDS and the rights of the child,* 2003.

—, *General Comment No. 1: The aims of education,* 2001.

United Nations Development Programme, *An Introduction into the Use of Human Rights Indicators for Development Programmes,* UNDP, New York, 2005.

United Nations Educational, Scientific and Cultural Organization, *EFA Global Monitoring Report*, UNESCO Publishing, Paris, annually, 2002–ongoing.

—, *Overcoming Exclusion through Inclusive Approaches to Education*, UNESCO, Paris, 2003.

—, *Education in a Multilingual World,* Education Position Paper, UNESCO, Paris, 2003.

—, *Education for All: Initiatives, issues and strategies*, Report of the Working Group on Education for All held at UNESCO Headquarters, 22-24 November 2000, UNESCO, Paris, 2001.

—, *Country Guidelines on the Preparation of National EFA Plans of Action,* UNESCO, Paris, 2000.

—, *World Education Report: The right to education,* UNESCO, Paris, 2000.

United Nations Educational, Scientific and Cultural Organization Bangkok, *Strengthening Inclusive Education by Applying a Rights-Based Approach to Education Programming*, UNESCO Bangkok, Bangkok, 2005.

—, *Guidelines for Implementing, Monitoring and Evaluating: Gender responsive EFA plans*, UNESCO Asia and Pacific Regional Bureau for Education, Bangkok, 2004.

United Nations Educational, Scientific and Cultural Organization/East Asia and Pacific Regional Office of the United Nations Children's Fund, *Government Action to Reduce Disparities in Education,* UNESCO/EAPRO, 2005.

United Nations Educational, Scientific and Cultural Organization/International Institute for Educational Planning, *The Guidebook for Planning Education in Emergencies and Reconstruction*, UNESCO/IEEP, Paris, 2005.

United Nations Educational, Scientific and Cultural Organization/Joint United Nations Programme on HIV/AIDS, *HIV/AIDS and Human Rights: Young people in action – A kit of ideas for youth organizations, UNESCO/UNAIDS,* 2001.

United Nations Educational, Scientific and Cultural Organization/Office of the United Nations High Commissioner for Human Rights, *United to Combat Racism: Selected articles and standard-setting instruments,* UNESCO, Paris, 2001.

United Nations Educational, Scientific and Cultural Organization/World Education Forum, *Thematic Study: Education in situations of emergency and crisis – Challenges for the new century*, UNESCO, Paris, 2000.

Wilson, Duncan, *Minority Rights in Education: Lessons for the European Union from Estonia, Latvia, Romania and the Former Yugoslav Republic of Macedonia,* Swedish International Development Agency, Stockholm, 2002.

Wright, Cream, 'HRBAP in Education: Global perspectives, challenges and options', draft paper for Second UNICEF Global Consultation on Human Rights-Based Approaches to Programming, Quito, September 2003.

# NORMATIVE AND STANDARD-SETTING INSTRUMENTS
*(in chronological order)*

## Conventions

The Geneva Conventions of 1949 – see especially articles 24, 50, 94 and 108 regarding education in conflict and under occupation

ILO Convention No. 111: Discrimination in Respect of Employment and Occupation, 1958

International Convention on the Elimination of All Forms of Racial Discrimination, 1965

International Covenant on Economic, Social and Cultural Rights, 1966

International Covenant on Civil and Political Rights, 1966

UNESCO Convention against Discrimination in Education, 1966

ILO Convention No. 138: Minimum Age of Employment, 1973

Convention on the Elimination of All Forms of Discrimination against Women, 1979

> Optional Protocol to the Convention on the Elimination of Discrimination against Women, 1999

UNESCO Convention on Technical and Vocational Education, 1989

ILO Convention No. 169: Indigenous and Tribal Peoples, 1989

Convention on the Rights of the Child, 1989

> Optional Protocol to the Convention on the Rights of the Child on the sale of children, child prostitution and child pornography, 2000

> Optional Protocol to the Convention on the Rights of the Child on the involvement of children in armed conflict, 2000

International Convention on the Protection of the Rights of All Migrant Workers and Members of Their Families, 1990

ILO Convention No. 182: Worst Forms of Child Labour, 1999

UNESCO Convention on the Protection and Promotion of Diversity in Cultural Expressions, 2005

Convention on the Rights of Persons with Disabilities, 2006

## Declarations, programmes and plans of action

Universal Declaration of Human Rights, 1948, see especially article 26

Declaration on the Protection of Women and Children in Emergency and Armed Conflict, 1974

World Declaration on Education for All, Meeting Basic Learning Needs, 1990

Vienna Declaration and Programme of Action of the United Nations World Conference on Human Rights, 1993

Plan of Action of the United Nations Decade for Human Rights Education, 1995

Declaration and Integrated Framework of Action on Education for Peace, Human Rights and Democracy, 1995

Beijing Declaration and Platform for Action, 1995

The Salamanca Statement and Framework for Action on Special Needs Education, 1995

Dakar Framework for Action, 'Education for All: Meeting our collective commitments', 2000

Millennium Development Declaration, 2000

Millennium Development Goals, 2000

Beijing +5 Outcome Document, 2000

Programme of Action of the World Conference against Racism, Racial Discrimination, Xenophobia and Related Intolerance, 2001

United Nations General Assembly Special Session 'A World Fit for Children', 2002

The Stamford Common Understanding on a Human Rights-based Approach to Development Cooperation, 2003

World Programme on Human Rights Education and the Plan of Action for the World Programme on Human Rights Education, 2004

Declaration of Amsterdam on the Right to and the Rights in Education, 2004

UN World Summit Outcome, 2005

Jakarta Declaration on the Right to Basic Education as a Fundamental Human Right and the Legal Framework for its Financing, 2005

Paris Declaration on Aid Effectiveness: Ownership, harmonisation, alignment, results and mutual accountability, 2005

Beijing + 10 Declaration, 2005

## WEB RESOURCES AND INITIATIVES

**CRED-PRO** – Child Rights Education for Professionals
<web.uvic.ca/iicrd/proj_credi.html>

**CRIN** – Childs Rights Information Network, rights-based programming
<www.crin.org/hrbap>

**Global Initiative to End All Corporal Punishment of Children**
<www.endcorporalpunishment.org>

**HREA** – Human Rights Education Association
<www.hrea.org>

**INEE** – Inter-Agency Network for Education in Emergencies
<www.ineesite.org>

**OHCHR** – Office of the High Commissioner for Human Rights
<www.ohchr.org>

> Committee on Economic, Social and Cultural Rights
> <www.ohchr.org/english/bodies/cescr>

> Committee on the Rights of the Child
> <www.ohchr.org/english/bodies/crc>

**Reports from UN Special Rapporteur** on the right to education
<www.ohchr.org/english/issues/education/rapporteur/annual.htm>

**RTE** –The Right to Education Project
<www.right-to-education.org>

**SFAI** – School Fee Abolition Initiative (launching September 2007)
<www.schoolfeeabolition.org>

**UN Secretary-General's Study on Violence against Children**
<www.violencestudy.org/r25>

**UNDP** – United Nations Development Programme

HURIST – Human Rights Strengthening Programme, with OHCHR
<www.undp.org/governance/programmes/hurist.htm>

HuRiTALK – Human Rights Policy Network
<www.undp.org/governance/programmes/huritalk.htm>

**UNESCO** – United Nations Educational, Scientific and Cultural Organization

Education portal, includes link to 'Global Monitoring Report'
<www.unesco.org/education>

The right to education
<www.portal.unesco.org/education/en/ev.php-URL_ID=9019&URL_DO=DO_
TOPIC&URL_SECTION=201.html>

**UNGEI** – The United Nations Girls' Education Initiative
<www.ungei.org>

**UNICEF** – United Nations Children's Fund

Basic education and gender equality
<www.unicef.org/girlseducation/index.php>

Convention on the Rights of the Child
<www.unicef.org/crc/index.html>

Innocenti Research Centre
<www.unicef-icdc.org>

# APPENDIX I: THE HUMAN RIGHTS-BASED APPROACH TO DEVELOPMENT COOPERATION

## Towards a common understanding among UN agencies[123]

## INTRODUCTION

The United Nations is founded on the principles of peace, justice, freedom and human rights. The Universal Declaration of Human Rights recognizes human rights as the foundation of freedom, justice and peace. The unanimously adopted Vienna Declaration and Programme of Action states that democracy, development and respect for human rights and fundamental freedoms are interdependent and mutually reinforcing.

In the UN Programme for Reform that was launched in 1997, the Secretary-General called on all entities of the UN system to mainstream human rights into their various activities and programmes within the framework of their respective mandates.

Since then a number of UN agencies have adopted a human rights-based approach to their development cooperation and have gained experiences in its operationalization. But each agency has tended to have its own interpretation of approach and how it should be operationalized. However, UN interagency collaboration at global and regional levels, and especially at the country level in relation to the CCA [Common Country Assessment] and UNDAF [United Nations Development Assistance Framework] processes, requires a common understanding of this approach and its implications for development programming. What follows is an attempt to arrive at such an understanding on the basis of those aspects of the human rights-based approach that are common to the policy and practice of the UN bodies that participated in the Interagency Workshop on a Human Rights based Approach in the context of UN reform 3–5 May 2003.

This Statement of Common Understanding specifically refers to a human rights-based approach to development cooperation and development programming by UN agencies.

## Common understanding

1.  All programmes of development co-operation, policies and technical assistance should further the realization of human rights as laid down in the Universal Declaration of Human Rights and other international human rights instruments.

2.  Human rights standards contained in, and principles derived from, the Universal Declaration of Human Rights and other international human rights instruments guide all development cooperation and programming in all sectors and in all phases of the programming process.

3.  Development cooperation contributes to the development of the capacities of 'duty-bearers' to meet their obligations and/or of 'rights-holders' to claim their rights.

1.  **All programmes of development co-operation, policies and technical assistance should further the realization of human rights as laid down in the Universal Declaration of Human Rights and other international human rights instruments.**

A set of programme activities that only incidentally contributes to the realization of human rights does not necessarily constitute a human rights-based approach to programming. In a human rights-based approach to programming and development cooperation, the aim of all activities is to contribute directly to the realization of one or several human rights.

2.  **Human rights standards contained in, and principles derived from, the Universal Declaration of Human Rights and other international human rights instruments guide all development cooperation and programming in all sectors and in all phases of the programming process.**

Human rights principles guide programming in all sectors, such as: health, education, governance, nutrition, water and sanitation, HIV/AIDS, employment and labour relations and social and economic security. This includes all development cooperation directed towards the achievement of the Millennium Development Goals and the Millennium Declaration. Consequently, human rights standards and principles guide both the CCA [Common Country Assessment] and the UNDAF [United Nations Development Assistance Framework].

Human rights principles guide all programming in all phases of the programming process, including assessment and analysis; programme planning and design (including setting of goals, objectives and strategies); and implementation, monitoring and evaluation.

Among these human rights principles are: universality and inalienability; indivisibility; interdependence and inter-relatedness; non-discrimination and equality; participation and inclusion; accountability and the rule of law. These principles are explained below.

- **Universality and Inalienability:** Human rights are universal and inalienable. All people everywhere in the world are entitled to them. The human person in whom they inhere cannot voluntarily give them up. Nor can others take them away from him or her. As stated in Article 1 of the UDHR, "All human beings are born free and equal in dignity and rights".
- **Indivisibility:** Human rights are indivisible. Whether of a civil, cultural, economic, political or social nature, they are all inherent to the dignity of every human person. Consequently, they all have equal status as rights and cannot be ranked, a priori, in a hierarchical order.
- **Inter-dependence and inter-relatedness:** The realization of one right often depends, wholly or in part, upon the realization of others. For instance, realization of the right to health may depend, in certain circumstances, on realization of the right to education or of the right to information.
- **Equality and Non-discrimination:** All individuals are equal as human beings and by virtue of the inherent dignity of each human person. All human beings are entitled to their human rights without discrimination of any kind, such as race, colour, sex, ethnicity, age, language, religion, political or other opinion, national or social origin, disability, property, birth or other status as explained by the human rights treaty bodies.
- **Participation and Inclusion:** Every person and all peoples are entitled to active, free and meaningful participation in, contribution to, and enjoyment of civil, economic, social, cultural and political development in which human rights and fundamental freedoms can be realized.
- **Accountability and Rule of Law:** States and other duty-bearers are answerable for the observance of human rights. In this regard, they have to comply with the legal norms and standards enshrined in human rights instruments. Where they fail to do so, aggrieved rights-holders are entitled to institute proceedings for appropriate redress before a competent court

or other adjudicator in accordance with the rules and procedures provided by law.

**3.    Programmes of development cooperation contribute to the development of the capacities of duty-bearers to meet their obligations and of 'rights-holders' to claim their rights.**

In a HRBA human rights determine the relationship between individuals and groups with valid claims (rights-holders) and State and non-state actors with correlative obligations (duty- bearers). It identifies *rights-holders* (and their entitlements) and corresponding *duty-bearers* (and their obligations) and works towards strengthening the capacities of rights-holders to make their claims, and of duty-bearers to meet their obligations.

## IMPLICATIONS OF A HUMAN RIGHTS-BASED APPROACH TO DEVELOPMENT PROGRAMMING OF UN AGENCIES

Experience has shown that the use of a human rights-based approach requires the use of good programming practices. However, the application of "good programming practices" does not by itself constitute a human rights-based approach and requires additional elements. The following elements are necessary, specific and unique to a human rights-based approach:

**a)**    Assessment and analysis in order to identify the human rights claims of rights-holders and the corresponding human rights obligations of duty-bearers as well as the immediate, underlying and structural causes of the non-realization of rights.

**b)**    Programmes assess the capacity of rights-holders to claim their rights and of duty-bearers to fulfil their obligations. They then develop strategies to build these capacities.

**c)**    Programmes monitor and evaluate both outcomes and processes guided by human rights standards and principles.

**d)**    Programming is informed by the recommendations of international human rights bodies and mechanisms.

Other elements of good programming practices that are also essential under an HRBA, include:

1. People are recognized as key actors in their own development, rather than passive recipients of commodities and services.

2. Participation is both a means and a goal.

3. Strategies are empowering, not disempowering.

4. Both outcomes and processes are monitored and evaluated.

5. Analysis includes all stakeholders.

6. Programmes focus on marginalized, disadvantaged and excluded groups.

7. The development process is locally owned.

8. Programmes aim to reduce disparity.

9. Both top-down and bottom-up approaches are used in synergy.

10. Situation analysis is used to identify immediate, underlying and basic causes of development problems.

11. Measurable goals and targets are important in programming.

12. Strategic partnerships are developed and sustained.

13. Programmes support accountability to all stakeholders.

# APPENDIX II: THE CONVENTION ON THE RIGHTS OF THE CHILD AND EDUCATION

All the following rights need to be addressed in the development of an education system that is consistent with the principles and standards of the United Nations Convention on the Rights of the Child (1989).

## 1. SPECIFIC EDUCATIONAL RIGHTS

**Article 28** – the right to education on the basis of equality of opportunity. This right needs to be realized through provision of compulsory and free primary education, and available and accessible secondary education.

**Article 29** – education needs to address the development of the child to his or her fullest potential and promote respect for human rights, the child's own culture and the natural environment and to promote values of understanding, peace, tolerance, equality and friendship. In other words, education must not be limited to the basic academic skills of writing, reading, mathematics and science.

## 2. GENERAL PRINCIPLES UNDERPINNING THE EDUCATION OF CHILDREN

**Article 2** – education must be provided without discrimination on any grounds.

**Article 3** – in all aspects of the education system, consideration of the child's best interests must be a primary consideration.

**Article 6** – education must seek to promote children's optimum development.

**Article 12** – children have the right to express their views on all aspects of their education, their views being given due weight in accordance with their age and maturity.

## 3. ADDITIONAL RELEVANT RIGHTS

**Article 7** – the right to birth registration. Many children are unable to enrol in school because they lack a birth certificate and proof of their age. Children with disabilities experience particular difficulties, as they are disproportionately vulnerable to non-registration.

**Articles 13–17** – the right to freedom of expression, thought, conscience and religion. Children also have the right to meet together with friends, to privacy and to information from a wide variety of sources.

**Article 19 (and 28.2)** – the right to protection from all forms of violence, injury, abuse, neglect or negligent treatment. Schools must also ensure that any discipline is administered in a way that does not undermine the dignity of a child.

**Article 23** – the right of children with disabilities to education, not only without discrimination and on the basis of equality of opportunity, but also that promotes their fullest possible social inclusion.

**Article 24** – the right to the best possible health.

**Article 30** – the right to enjoy their own culture, language and religion.

**Article 31** – the right to rest, play, recreation, leisure and to enjoy and take part in cultural life and the arts.

**Article 32** – the right to protection from economic exploitation or hazardous work.

**Article 34** – the right to protection from sexual exploitation and abuse.

**Article 42** – the right to know about the Convention on the Rights of the Child and its implications for their lives.

# APPENDIX III: OVERVIEW OF GLOBAL GOALS PERTAINING TO EDUCATION

| Global Commitments | 2005 | 2010 | 2015 |
|---|---|---|---|
| **Education for All World Education Forum – Dakar Goals** | • Eliminate gender disparities in primary and secondary education by 2005, with a focus on ensuring girls' full and equal access to and achievement in basic education of good quality. | | • Achieve gender equality in education by 2015, with a focus on ensuring girls' full and equal access to and achievement in basic education of good quality.<br><br>• Ensure that by 2015 all children, particularly girls, children in difficult circumstances and those belonging to ethnic minorities, have access to and complete, free and compulsory primary education of good quality.<br><br>• Achieve a 50 per cent improvement in levels of adult literacy by 2015, especially for women, and equitable access to basic and continuing education for all adults. |
| **World Fit for Children**<br><br>**Specific goals of Plan of Action** | • Eliminate gender disparities in primary and secondary education by 2005, with a focus on ensuring girls' full and equal access to and achievement in basic education of good quality. | • Reduce the number of primary school-aged children who are out of school by 50 per cent and increase net primary school enrolment or participation in alternative, good quality primary education programmes to at least 90 per cent by 2010. | • Achieve gender equality in education by 2015, with a focus on ensuring girls' full and equal access to and achievement in basic education of good quality.<br><br>• Achieve a 50 per cent improvement in levels of adult literacy by 2015, especially for women.<br><br>• Ensure by 2015 that all children have access to and complete primary education that is free, compulsory and of good quality.<br><br>• Achieve a 50 per cent improvement in levels of adult literacy by 2015, especially for women. |

| Global Commitments | 2005 | 2010 | 2015 |
|---|---|---|---|
| **Millennium Development Goals** | **3. Promote gender equality and empower women**<br><br>• Eliminate gender disparity in primary and secondary education preferably by 2005 and at all levels by 2015. | | **2. Achieve universal primary education**<br><br>• Ensure that, by 2015, all boys and girls complete a full course of primary schooling.<br><br>**3. Promote gender equality and empower women**<br><br>• Eliminate gender disparity in primary and secondary education preferably by 2005 and at all levels by 2015. |
| **Summit of the Americas – Education Action Plan: General objectives** | | • That by the year 2010, 100 per cent of children complete quality primary education.<br><br>• That at least 75 per cent of young people have access to quality secondary education, with increasing graduation rates and lifelong learning opportunities for the general population. | |

| | GOALS THAT HAVE A CROSS-CUTTING TIME FRAME | |
|---|---|---|
| **Education for All**<br><br>**World Education Forum – Dakar Goals** | • Expand and improve comprehensive early childhood care and education, especially for the most vulnerable and disadvantaged children.<br><br>• Ensure that the learning needs of all young people and adults are met through equitable access to appropriate learning and life-skills programmes.<br><br>• Improve all aspects of the quality of education and ensure excellence of all so that recognized and measurable learning outcomes are achieved by all, especially in literacy, numeracy and essential life skills. | |
| **World Fit for Children**<br><br>**Specific goals of Plan of Action** | • Expand and improve comprehensive early childhood care and education, for girls and boys, especially for the most vulnerable and disadvantaged children.<br><br>• Aim at the progressive provision of secondary education.<br><br>• Ensure that the learning needs of all young people are met through access to appropriate learning and life skills programmes.<br><br>• Improve all aspects of the quality of education so that children and young people achieve recognized and measurable learning outcomes, especially in numeracy, literacy and essential life skills. | |

# APPENDIX IV: A CHECKLIST FOR ACTION: STATE OBLIGATIONS IN ENSURING THE RIGHT TO EDUCATION

The following actions are necessary on the part of States if they are to fulfil the Education for All goals and ensure the right to a quality education for all children that is respectful of their rights. These actions can also serve as benchmarks or indicators for monitoring the implementation of human rights-based education:

## OVERARCHING MEASURES

☐ Ratification of all relevant human rights conventions (including the Convention on the Rights of the Child, the Convention against Discrimination in Education, the Convention on the Elimination of All Forms of Discrimination against Women, the International Covenant on Economic, Social and Cultural Rights and the International Convention on the Rights of Persons with Disabilities).

☐ Consideration of relevant recommendations from treaty bodies.

☐ Establishment of multisectoral approaches to coordinate and implement the right to education across all stages of the life cycle.

☐ Review of all relevant legislation to ensure consistency with the right of universal access to education – for example, minimum age of marriage, non-discrimination, child labour, compulsory years of education, birth registration, protection from all forms of violence, exclusion of children with disabilities.

☐ Devolution of responsibility for education, accompanied by capacity-building, access to budgets and systems for ensuring local accountability and involvement.

☐ Commitment to transparency, accountability, access to justice and stakeholder participation in the provision of education.

# ACCESS TO EDUCATION

## Adopting a life-cycle approach

☐ Budgetary allocation for the provision of early childhood education.

☐ Measures to promote the introduction of early childhood education and appropriate transitioning strategies with parent and family involvement.

☐ Measures to develop the accessibility of secondary education to every child, for example, by offering financial assistance to those in need.

☐ Full commitment to universal access to free secondary education.

☐ Consistency of legal ages for completion of compulsory education and admission into full time employment.

☐ Legislation to raise the minimum age of employment where this falls below 15 years.

## Providing available and accessible schools

☐ Legislation specifying the minimum number of years of free and compulsory education.

☐ Legislation defining the entitlement to education in terms of numbers of hours and weeks of teaching, qualifications of teachers, etc.

☐ Budgetary analysis and allocation to ensure sufficiency of provision in accordance with the school-aged population – commitment of 20 per cent of government revenues to education.

☐ Measures to ensure accessibility of schools for all children, including the physical environment, provision of appropriate facilities and resources for children with disabilities, water and sanitation facilities, etc.

☐ Measures to promote school attendance and reduce school drop out, including consideration of location of schools, and respect for children's differing capacities and their culture, language and religion.

☐   Measures to ensure equality of access to education for children in situations of emergency, including extreme poverty, HIV and AIDS and armed conflict.

☐   Review of all aspects of education supplies, including textbooks, notebooks, etc., their manufacture and supply, logistics and distribution, as well as taxation and import tariffs if not produced in the country.

☐   Establishment of robust, reliable educational information systems to provide disaggregated data for planning, budgeting and assessment of performance against standards.

☐   Disaggregation of data on enrolment, attendance, completion and attainment according to socio-economic status, gender, disability, ethnicity, geographic location, etc.

## Removing the economic barriers to education

☐   Inclusion of specific measures such as stipends and cash transfers in national plans of action and poverty reduction strategy papers.

☐   Abolition of fees for primary education.

☐   Collaboration with the non-formal education sector to promote and facilitate access to education including other learning spaces and opportunities, and effective transitions into formal education.

## Promoting inclusion and ending discrimination

☐   Introduction of legislation to prohibit all forms of discrimination in relation to access to education.

☐   Measures to overcome all forms of direct and indirect discrimination impeding access to education, including sensitization of families and communities to the universal right to education.

☐   Introduction of policies to address girls' right to education.

☐ Introduction of inclusive education, including flexible approaches to timetabling to accommodate working children and agricultural harvests, and support and facilities to accommodate the differing learning needs of children with disabilities.

☐ Introduction of legislation and policies to ensure universal access to birth registration.

☐ Consultation with local communities to identify the barriers faced and strategies for overcoming them.

# QUALITY EDUCATION

## Providing a broad, relevant and inclusive curriculum

☐ Broad-based curriculum that equips children with numeracy and literacy, as well as a wider range of subjects including science, humanities, sport, the arts and opportunities for play consistent with the right to optimum development.

☐ The inclusion of human rights education within an environment that reflects human rights principles and practices.

☐ Review of curriculum to eliminate gender, racial and other bias.

☐ Bilingual or multilingual education provided to children not familiar with the language of instruction in schools.

## Developing rights-based learning and assessment

☐ Introduction of child-friendly schools that are rooted in a culture of respect for human rights and have regard to participatory and inclusive teaching methods that take account of the evolving capacities of the child.

☐ Measures to promote the active participation of parents and members of the local community at all levels of the school.

☐ Provision of the appropriate level of resources to schools – books, equipment, furniture and improved teacher-student ratios.

☐ Assessment procedures consistent with respect for the dignity of the child and designed to promote self-esteem and optimum development.

## Ensuring adequate training, support and respect for teachers

☐ Introduction of initial and in-service training for teachers consistent with working in child-friendly schools.

☐ Introduction of measures to protect the rights of teachers – levels of pay, management support, etc.

## Introducing child-friendly, safe and healthy learning environments

☐ Introduction of minimum health and safety standards in education – including health and safety management and the teaching of health and safety in the curriculum.

☐ Number and frequency of inspections of schools to ensure conformity with minimum standards.

☐ Every school familiar with requirements on health and safety in respect of buildings, play areas, first aid, child protection systems.

☐ Provision of packages of health care delivered through community-based school programmes, including nutrition, screening, health checks, malaria prevention and attention to children affected by HIV/AIDS.

# RESPECT FOR RIGHTS IN EDUCATION

## Respecting identity

☐ Bilingual or multilingual education provided to children not familiar with the language of instruction in schools.

☐ Consultations with local communities on measures to ensure respect for religion, culture and language.

## Ensuring children's participation

☐ Systems for student participation at all levels throughout schools.

☐ Involvement of children in development of school policies on issues relating to, for example, non-discrimination, disciplinary codes.

☐ Evidence of institutionalized consultation between children, community and minority groups, and ministries of education and other bodies responsible for realizing the right to education.

## Protecting integrity

☐ Provision of legislation, training and practice to end physical and humiliating punishment of children.

☐ Review of schools' disciplinary rules and practices.

☐ Introduction of mechanisms for challenging rights violations.

☐ Support and training for teachers in ending physical punishment and introducing strategies for non-violent conflict resolution.

# APPENDIX V: WORLD PROGRAMME FOR HUMAN RIGHTS EDUCATION, PLAN OF ACTION 2005–2007

The World Programme for Human Rights Education was proclaimed by the United Nations on 10 December 2004 to advance the implementation of human rights education programmes in all sectors (General Assembly resolution 59/113). It provides a collective framework for action based on human rights education principles agreed on by the international community. Its aims are to promote a common understanding of the basic principles and methodologies, to support existing initiatives, to build on the achievements of the United Nations Decade for Human Rights Education (1995–2004) and to provide an incentive to continue and expand these achievements – as well as develop new initiatives – through partnership and cooperation at all levels.

A Plan of Action for the First Phase (2005–2007) of the World Programme, which focuses on primary and secondary school systems, was adopted by the General Assembly on 14 July 2005. Developed by a large group of education specialists and human rights practitioners from all parts of the world, the Plan promotes a holistic, rights-based approach to human rights education in the school system. This includes both 'human rights *through* education' (ensuring that all the components and processes of education – including curricula, materials, methods and training – are conducive to the learning of human rights) and 'human rights *in* education' (ensuring that the human rights of all members of the school community are respected).

Although many factors contribute to the effective integration of this approach in primary and secondary schools, research and experience worldwide have identified five key components for success: (1) educational policies, (2) policy implementation, (3) the learning environment, (4) teaching and learning and (5) education and professional development of school personnel. Practical guidance on how to implement these five components in the school system is provided in an appendix to the Plan of Action.[124]

The Plan of Action proposes four stages for developing a national implementation strategy:

1. **Analysis of the current situation of human rights education in the school system.**

2. **Setting of priorities and development of a national implementation strategy.**

3. **Implementation and monitoring of activities.**

4. **Evaluation.**

In January 2006, the Director-General of the United Nations Educational, Scientific and Cultural Organization (UNESCO) and the United Nations High Commissioner for Human Rights jointly addressed personal letters to the Ministers of Education in all United Nations Member States. The letters encouraged implementation of the Plan of Action at the national level and asked the Ministers to nominate a national coordinating unit for the World Programme, as well as to inform the Office of the High Commissioner on Human Rights (OHCHR) and UNESCO of the overall initiatives undertaken to implement the plan. A follow-up strategy of regional meetings was initiated by UNESCO Headquarters in partnership with regional offices with the aim of encouraging national authorities to assume an active role in analysing the situation of human rights education in the school system, and to identify and overcome any cultural particularities and constraints Member States may face.

In accordance with the Plan of Action, a United Nations Inter-Agency Coordinating Committee on Human Rights Education in the School System was established in 2006 to coordinate international activities supporting the integration of human rights education in national school systems, as well as to ensure UN system-wide support to national implementation strategies. The Committee is composed of UNESCO, OHCHR, the United Nations Children's Fund (UNICEF), the United Nations Development Programme (UNDP), the International Labour Organization (ILO), the Joint United Nations Programme on HIV/AIDS (UNAIDS), the United Nations Population Fund (UNFPA), the United Nations Refugee Agency (UNHCR), the United Nations Relief and Works Agency for Palestine Refugees in the Near East (UNRWA) and the World Bank.

The Coordinating Committee met for the second time on 20–21 February 2007 in Geneva. The meeting was intended to analyse opportunities and challenges to further involve UN agencies at the country level in assisting the implementation of the first phase of the World Programme for Human Rights Education; to explore approaches/initiatives to further engage Member States in implementing the Plan of Action; to review methods to monitor national progress, based on existing UN mechanisms; and to examine possible cooperation with other inter-agency initiatives related to human rights/education. At the conclusion of the first phase of the World Programme, each country will evaluate its actions and report on these to the Coordinating Committee, which will then prepare a final report for the General Assembly in 2008.

**Sources:** United Nations, 'Revised draft plan of action for the first phase (2005–2007) of the World Programme for Human Rights Education', A/59/525/Rev.1, UN General Assembly Fifty-ninth session, 2 March 2005, New York, <www.ohchr.org/english/issues/education/docs/A.59.525.Rev.1.pdf>; United Nations, 'Plan of Action, World Programme for Human Rights Education, First Phase', UNESCO/OHCHR, New York and Geneva, 2006, <http://unesdoc.unesco.org/images/0014/001478/147853e.pdf>; and Second Meeting of the United Nations Inter-Agency Coordinating Committee on Human Rights Education in the School System, 'Summary Report, Human Rights Education in the Primary and Secondary School Systems, 1st Phase (2005–2007) of the World Programme for Human Rights Education', Geneva, 20-21 February 2007, <www.ohchr.org/english/issues/education/training/docs/SummaryofSecondmeeting.pdf>, all accessed 2 July 2007.

# APPENDIX VI: PRACTICE STANDARDS IN CHILDREN'S PARTICIPATION

(Quoted with permission from International Save the Children Alliance, *Practice Standards in Children's Participation*, Save the Children UK, London, 2005.)

## WHAT ARE PRACTICE STANDARDS?

Practice standards [also known as 'minimum quality standards' or 'key elements'] are statements that describe an expected level of performance. These practice standards state what children and others can expect of Save the Children's practice in child participation. They are designed to apply to all Save the Children's child participation work and represent minimum expectations of the ways in which staff will behave and operate.

These practice standards have been developed through years of experience supporting children's participation at both the local and global levels. This final set of standards is based on feedback and consultations with Save the Children staff, partner organisations and children in various countries and community settings. ... Each standard is accompanied by a set of criteria that can be used as indicators to see whether or not the standard is being met. ...

## STANDARD 1: AN ETHICAL APPROACH – TRANSPARENCY, HONESTY AND ACCOUNTABILITY

### What
Adult organisations and workers are committed to ethical participatory practice and to the primacy of children's best interests.

### Why
There are inevitable imbalances in power and status between adults and children. An ethical approach is needed in order for children's participation to be genuine and meaningful.

## How to meet this standard

- Girls and boys are able to freely express their views and opinions and have them treated with respect.
- There is clarity of purpose about children's participation and honesty about its parameters. Children understand how much impact they can have on decision-making and who will make the final decision.
- The roles and responsibilities of all involved (children and adults) are clearly outlined, understood and agreed upon.
- Clear goals and targets are agreed upon with the children concerned.
- Children are provided with, and have access to, relevant information regarding their involvement.
- Children are involved from the earliest possible stage and are able to influence the design and content of participatory processes.
- 'Outside' adults involved in any participatory processes are sensitised to working with children, clear about their role and willing to listen and learn.
- Organisations and workers are accountable to children for the commitments they make.
- Where the process of involvement requires representation from a wider group of children, the selection of representatives will be based on principles of democracy and non-discrimination.
- The barriers and challenges that participating children may have faced in other spheres of their lives are considered and discussed with the children involved to reduce any potential negative impacts from their participation.

## STANDARD 2: CHILDREN'S PARTICIPATION IS RELEVANT AND VOLUNTARY

### What
Children participate in processes and address issues that affect them – either directly or indirectly – and have the choice as to whether to participate or not.

### Why
Children's participation should build on their personal knowledge – the information and insights that children have about their own lives, their communities and the issues that affect them. Recognising their other commitments, children participate on their own terms and for lengths of time chosen by them.

## How to meet this standard

- The issues are of real relevance to the children being involved and draw upon their knowledge, skills and abilities.
- Children are involved in setting the criteria for selection and representation for participation.
- Children have time to consider their involvement and processes are established to ensure that they are able to give their personal, informed consent to their participation.
- Children's participation is voluntary and they can withdraw at any time they wish.
- Children are involved in ways, at levels and at a pace appropriate to their capacities and interests.
- Children's other time commitments are respected and accommodated (eg, to home, work and school).
- Ways of working and methods of involvement incorporate, and build on, supportive local structures, knowledge and practice and take into consideration social, economic, cultural and traditional practices.
- Support from key adults in children's lives (eg, parents/guardians, teachers) is gained to ensure wider encouragement and assistance for the participation of girls and boys.

## STANDARD 3: A CHILD-FRIENDLY, ENABLING ENVIRONMENT

### What
Children experience a safe, welcoming and encouraging environment for their participation.

### Why
The quality of children's participation and their ability to benefit from it are strongly influenced by the efforts made to create a positive environment for their participation.

## How to implement this standard

- Ways of working build the self-esteem and self-confidence of boys and girls of different ages and abilities so that they feel they are able to contribute and that they have valid experience and views to contribute.
- Methods of involvement are developed in partnership with children so that they reflect their preferred mediums of expression.
- Sufficient time and resources are made available for quality participation and children are properly supported to prepare for their participation.
- Adults (including children's own parents/guardians) are sensitised to understand the value of children's participation and are enabled to play a positive role in supporting it (eg, through awareness-raising, reflection and capacity building).
- Child-friendly meeting places are used where girls and boys feel relaxed, comfortable and have access to the facilities they need. The meeting places must be accessible to children with disabilities.
- Organisational or official procedures are designed/modified to facilitate (rather than intimidate) children and make less experienced boys and girls feel welcome.
- Support is provided where necessary to share information and/or build skills and capacity to enable children, individually and collectively, to participate effectively.
- Children are asked what information they need and accessible information is shared with children in good time, in child-friendly formats and in languages that the children understand, including children with visual or hearing impairments.
- In situations where children meet with different native/first languages, access to written information and professional interpretation is provided that allows for children's full participation in discussions.
- Non-technical language is used in all discussions involving children and/or all jargon or technical terms are clearly explained.

# STANDARD 4: EQUALITY OF OPPORTUNITY

## What
Child participation work challenges and does not reinforce existing patterns of discrimination and exclusion. It encourages those groups of children who typically suffer discrimination and who are often excluded from activities to be involved in participatory processes.

## Why
Children, like adults, are not a homogeneous group and participation provides for equality of opportunity for all, regardless of the child's age, race, colour, sex, language, religion, political or other opinion, national, ethnic or social origin, property, disability, birth or other status (or those of his or her parents/guardians).

## How to implement this standard

- All children have an equal chance to participate and systems are developed to ensure that children are not discriminated against because of age, race, colour, sex, language, religion, political or other opinion, national, ethnic or social origin, property, disability, birth or other status.
- Children's involvement aims to include all rather than a few, this could mean reaching out to children in their local settings rather than inviting representatives to a central point.
- Participatory practice with children is flexible enough to respond to the needs, expectations and situation of different groups of children – and to regularly re-visit these concerns.
- The age range, gender and abilities of children are taken into account in the way participation is organised (eg, in the way information is presented).
- Those working with children are able to facilitate an environment that is non-discriminatory and inclusive.
- No assumptions are made about what different groups of children can and cannot do.
- All children are given an equal opportunity to voice their opinions and have their contributions reflected in any outcomes of a participatory process, including in processes that involve both children and adults.
- If there is a limit to how many children can participate, children themselves select from among their peers those who will represent them in participatory initiatives based on the principles of democracy and inclusion.
- Influential adults are engaged to gain family and community support for the participation of discriminated-against groups.

# STANDARD 5: STAFF ARE EFFECTIVE AND CONFIDENT

## What

Adult staff and managers involved in supporting/facilitating children's participation are trained and supported to do their jobs to a high standard.

## Why

Adult workers can only encourage genuine children's participation effectively and confidently if they have the necessary understandings and skills.

## How to implement this standard

- All staff and managers are sensitised to children's participation and understand the organisational commitment to children's participation.
- Staff are provided with appropriate training, tools and other development opportunities in participatory practice to enable them to work effectively and confidently with children of different ages and abilities.
- Staff are properly supported and supervised, and evaluate their participation practice.
- Specific technical skill or expertise (eg, in communication, facilitation, conflict resolution or multi-cultural working) is built up through a combination of recruitment, selection, staff development and practice exchange.
- Relations between individual staff, and between staff and management, model appropriate behaviour, treating each other with respect and honesty.
- Support is provided for managers and staff for whom children's participation represents a significant personal or cultural change, without this being regarded as a problem.
- Staff are able to express any views or anxieties about involving children in the expectation that these will be addressed in a constructive way.

## STANDARD 6: PARTICIPATION PROMOTES THE SAFETY AND PROTECTION OF CHILDREN

### What

Child protection policies and procedures form an essential part of participatory work with children. *Please note: Save the Children staff should use these practice standards in conjunction with the organisation's child protection policy.*

### Why

Organisations have a duty of care to children with whom they work and everything must be done to minimise the risk to children of abuse and exploitation or other negative consequences of their participation.

### How to implement this standard

- The protection rights of children are paramount in the way children's participation is planned and organised.
- Children involved in participation work are aware of their right to be safe from abuse and know where to go for help if needed.
- Skilled, knowledgeable staff are delegated to address and coordinate child protection issues during participatory processes.
- Staff organising a participatory process have a child protection strategy that is specific to each process. The strategy must be well communicated and understood by all staff involved in the process.
- Safeguards are in place to minimise risks and prevent abuse (eg, children are adequately supervised and protected at all times; risk assessments are in place for residential activities away from home; children are protected from abuse from other children).
- Staff recognise their legal and ethical obligations and responsibilities (eg, in respect of their own behaviour or what to do if they are told about the inappropriate behaviour of others). A system for reporting critical incidents is in place and understood by all staff.
- Child protection procedures recognise the particular risks faced by some groups of children and the extra barriers they face to obtaining help.
- Careful assessment is made of the risks associated with children's participation in speaking out, campaigning or advocacy. Depending upon the risks identified, steps may be needed to protect children's identity or to provide follow-up measures to give protection (eg, to ensure their safe reintegration into their communities).

- Consent is obtained for the use of all information provided by children and information identified as confidential needs to be safeguarded at all times.
- A formal complaints procedure is set up to allow children involved in participatory activities to make a complaint in confidence about any issue concerning their involvement. Information about the complaints procedure is accessible to children in relevant languages and formats.
- No photographs, videos or digital images of a child can be taken or published without that child's explicit consent for a specific use.
- Unless otherwise agreed, it must not be possible to trace information back to individual/groups of children.
- Responsibilities relating to liability, safety, travel and medical insurance are clearly delegated and effectively planned for.

## STANDARD 7: ENSURING FOLLOW-UP AND EVALUATION

### What
Respect for children's involvement is indicated by a commitment to provide feedback and/or follow-up and to evaluate the quality and impact of children's participation.

### Why
It is important that children understand what has been the outcome from their participation and how their contribution has been used. It is also important that, where appropriate, they are given the opportunity to participate in follow-up processes or activities. As a key stakeholder, children are an integral part of monitoring and evaluation processes.

### How to implement this standard

- Children are supported to participate in follow-up and evaluation processes.
- Follow-up and evaluation are addressed during the planning stages, as an integral part of any participation initiative.
- Children are supported and encouraged to share their participatory experiences with peer groups, local communities, organisations and projects with which they may be involved.
- Children are given rapid and clear feedback on the impact of their involvement, the outcome of any decisions, next steps and the value of their involvement.

- Feedback reaches all children involved.
- Children are asked about their satisfaction with the participation process and for their views on ways in which it could be improved.
- The results of monitoring and evaluation are communicated back to the children involved in an accessible and child-friendly way, and their feedback is taken into account in future participation work.
- Mistakes identified through evaluation are acknowledged and commitments given about how lessons learned will be used to improve participatory processes in the future.
- Adults will evaluate how they have translated and implemented children's priorities and recommendations into their policies, strategies and programmes.
- Sustainability of support is discussed with children. Adults will provide clear feedback to children regarding the extent/limit of their commitment to support children's ongoing initiatives and organisations. If ongoing support is not possible, adults will provide children with resources and support to make contact with other agencies who can support them.

# ENDNOTES

1   Tomaševski, Katarina, *Manual on Rights-Based Education: Global human rights requirements made simple*, UNESCO Bangkok, Bangkok, 2004.

2   Committee on the Rights of the Child, 'General Comment No. 1: The aims of education, article 29 (1) (2001)', CRC/GC/2001/1, 2001.

3   Committee on Economic, Social and Cultural Rights, 'General Comment No. 13: The right to education (article 13)', E/C.12/1999/10, December 1999, para. 1.

4   Ibid.

5   United Nations Educational, Scientific and Cultural Organization, 'Regional Overview: Latin America and the Caribbean', prepared for the *EFA Global Monitoring Report 2007*, UNESCO, Paris, 2006, p. 2.

6   United Nations Educational, Scientific and Cultural Organization, *EFA Global Monitoring Report 2007: Strong foundations — Early childhood care and education,* UNESCO, Paris, 2006; United Nations Children's Fund, *Progress for Children: A World Fit for Children statistical review,* UNICEF, New York, forthcoming, December 2007.

7   Watkins, Kevin, *The Oxfam Education Report,* Oxfam GB, London, 2000, p. 105.

8   Santos Pais, Marta, 'The Convention on the Rights of the Child', in Office of the High Commissioner for Human Rights, United Nations Institute for Training and Research, and United Nations Staff College Project, *Manual on Human Rights Reporting under Six Major International Human Rights Instruments*, United Nations, Geneva, 1997, p. 427.

9   United Nations Children's Fund, *The State of the World's Children 2007: Women and children – The double dividend of gender equality*, UNICEF, New York, 2006, pp. x, 7.

10  United Nations Girls' Education Initiative, 'Girls Too!: Education for all', UNGEI Fact Sheet, 2006, <www.ungei.org>, accessed 28 June 2007.

11  Save the Children, *Ending Physical and Humiliating Punishment of Children: Making it happen,* International Save the Children Alliance, Stockholm, 2005, pp. 16–17.

12  Department for International Development et al., *HIV/AIDS and Education: A strategic approach*, International Institute for Educational Planning/United Nations Educational, Scientific and Cultural Organization, Paris, May 2003, pp. 18, 20.

13  Save the Children, *Child Rights Programming: How to apply rights-based approaches to programming*, 2nd ed., Save the Children Sweden, Stockholm, 2005, p. 41.

14  Frankovits, André, *The Human Rights-based Approach and the United Nations System*, United Nations Educational, Scientific and Cultural Organization, Paris, 2006, p. 20.

15  Tomaševski, Katarina, *Manual on Rights-based Education*, op. cit., p. 49.

16  Committee on the Rights of the Child, 'General Comment No. 1: The aims of education, article 29 (1) (2001)', CRC/GC/2001/1, 2001, para. 1.

17  Graham-Brown, Sarah, 'The Role of the Curriculum', Chapter 6, *Education Rights and Minorities*, Minority Rights Group, London, 1994, p. 27.

18  Committee on Economic, Social and Cultural Rights, 'General Comment No. 13: The right to education (article 13)', E/C.12/1999/10, December 1999, para. 1.

19 Article 26(3) of the Universal Declaration of Human Rights, article 18(4) of the International Covenant on Civil and Political Rights and article 2 of Protocol No.1 to the European Convention on Human Rights.

20 Boyden Jo, Birgitta Ling and William Myers, *What Works for Working Children*, Rädda Barnen, Stockholm, and UNICEF International Child Development Centre, Florence, 1998, pp. 9–11.

21 United Nations Educational, Scientific and Cultural Organization, *EFA Global Monitoring Report 2005: The quality imperative,* UNESCO Publishing, Paris, 2004, *p. 121.* CONFEMEN stands for *Conférence des ministres de l'Education des pays ayant le français en partage* (Conference of Education Ministers of French-speaking Countries).

22 Ibid., p. 122.

23 United Nations Children's Fund, 'A League Table of Disadvantage in Rich Nations', *Innocenti Report Card No. 4,* UNICEF Innocenti Research Centre, Florence, November 2002, p. 7.

24 Committee on the Rights of the Child, 'General Comment No. 1: The aims of education, article 29 (1) (2001)', CRC/GC/2001/1, 2001, para. 9.

25 United Nations Educational, Scientific and Cultural Organization, *EFA Global Monitoring Report 2007: Strong foundations – Early childhood care and education,* UNESCO, Paris, 2006, p. 12.

26 Save the Children, 'What's the Difference? The impact of early childhood development programs', Save the Children, Kathmandu, 2003, pp. 21, 32.

27 Hodgkin, Rachel, and Peter Newell, *Implementation Handbook on the Convention on the Rights of the Child*, United Nations Children's Fund, New York, 2002, p. 379.

28 Committee on Economic, Social and Cultural Rights, 'General Comment No. 13: The right to education (article 13)', E/C.12/1999/10, December 1999, para. 50.

29 Ibid.

30 United Nations Educational, Scientific and Cultural Organization, Convention against Discrimination in Education, 14 December 1960, articles 3, 4.

31 United Nations Children's Fund, *The State of the World's Children 2004: Girls, education and development*, UNICEF, New York, 2003, pp. 71, 84, 87.

32 United Nations Educational, Scientific and Cultural Organization, *EFA Global Monitoring Report 2005: The quality imperative,* UNESCO Publishing, Paris, 2004, p. 28.

33 Thomas Hammarberg, former vice-chair of the Committee on the Rights of the Child, quoted in Centre for Studies on Inclusive Education, 'Inclusive Education: A framework for change – National and international perspectives', CSIE, Bristol, 1997, p. 6.

34 Committee on the Rights of the Child, 'General Comment No. 1: The aims of education, article 29 (1) (2001)', CRC/GC/2001/1, 2001, para. 2.

35 Ibid, para. 9.

36 Ibid, para 8.

37 Ibid, para. 12.

38 Hodgkin and Newell, op, cit., p. 159.

39 Lansdown, Gerison, *Betrayal of Trust: An overview of Save the Children's findings on children's experience of physical and humiliating punishment, child sexual abuse and violence when in conflict with the law*, Save the Children, Stockholm, 2006, pp. 33–34.

40  Save the Children, *Ending Physical and Humiliating Punishment of Children: Making it happen*, International Save the Children Alliance, 2005, p. 40.

41  Committee on Economic, Social and Cultural Rights, 'General Comment No. 13: The right to education (article 13)', E/C.12/1999/10, December 1999, paras. 43, 44, 50.

42  Santos Pais, Marta, op. cit., pp. 419–423.

43  Committee on Social, Economic and Cultural Rights, 'General Comment No. 3', 14/12/90, 1990, para. 10; Committee on the Rights of the Child, 'General Comment No. 5', CRC/GC/2003/527, November 2003, para. 8.

44  Committee on Economic, Social and Cultural Rights, 'Substantive Issues Arising in the Implementation of the International Covenant on Economic, Social and Cultural Rights', E/C.12/2001/15, December 2001, para. 12.

45  Virtue John, 'Evaluation of the Role of UNICEF on Education Sector Wide Approaches in Eastern and Southern Africa: Business as usual or making a difference…?', study commissioned by UNICEF, Eastern and Southern Africa Regional Office, November 2005, p. 1.

46  Tomaševski, Katarina, *Manual on Rights-based Education*, op. cit., p. 29.

47  Development Assistance Committee/Organisation for Economic Co-operation and Development, *Gender Equality in Sector Wide Approaches: A reference guide*, OECD, Paris, 2002, pp. 3–4.

48  Fast Track Initiative, *Education for All – Fast Track Initiative: Framework*, World Bank, Washington, D.C., 2004, annex 1, p. 15.

49  Hodgkin and Newell, op. cit., p. 51.

50  International Save the Children Alliance Europe Group, *Children, Economics and the EU: Towards child friendly policies*, Save the Children, Stockholm, 2000, p. 18.

51  Furniss, Elaine, *Assessing Learning Achievement*, United Nations Children's Fund, New York, 2003, p. 2.

52  Save the Children, *So You Want to Involve Children in Research? A toolkit supporting children's meaningful and ethical participation in research relating to violence against children*, Save the Children Sweden, Stockholm, 2004, p. 10.

53  Committee on the Rights of the Child, 'General Comment No. 1: The aims of education, article 29 (1) (2001)', CRC/GC/2001/1, 2001, para. 23.

54  United Nations Educational, Scientific and Cultural Organization, *EFA Global Monitoring Report 2002: Is the world on track?*, UNESCO, Paris, 2002, p. 106.

55  Melchiorre Angela, *At What age?…are school children employed, married and taken to court?*, 2nd ed., Right to Education Project, Lund, 2004, p. 5.

56  United Nations, 'Programme of Action of the World Conference against Racism, Racial Discrimination, Xenophobia and Related Intolerance', 2001, A/CONF.189/12, para. 122.

57  Hodgkin and Newell, op. cit., p. 281.

58  Commission on Human Rights, 'Report of the Special Rapporteur, Katarina Tomaševski, submitted pursuant to resolution 2002/23', E/CN.4/2003/913, December 2002, para. 23.

59  Sakurai, Riho, 'Child Labour and Education', background paper prepared for the *Education for All Global Monitoring Report 2007*, United Nations Educational, Scientific and Cultural Organization, 2006, p. 28.

60   Melchiorre, op. cit., p. 5.

61   United Nations Convention on the Rights of the Child, article 32; and International Labour Organization Convention 182.

62   United Nations Children's Fund, *The 'Rights' Start to Life: A statistical analysis of birth registration*, UNICEF, New York, 2005, pp. 3–4.

63   United Nations Children's Fund, 'Factsheet: Birth registration', UNICEF, <www.unicef.org/newsline/2003/03fsbirthregistration.htm>, accessed 29 June 2007.

64   For detailed information on action to end physical punishment, see Harper, Kate, et al., *Ending Physical and Humiliating Punishment of Children: Manual for Action*, Save the Children Sweden/International Save the Children Alliance, Stockholm, 2005.

65   Pinheiro, Paulo Sérgio, *The World Report on Violence Against Children*, Report by the Independent Expert for the United Nations Secretary-General's Study on Violence against Children, Office of the United Nations High Commissioner for Human Rights, United Nations Children's Fund and the World Health Organization. Geneva, 2006, pp. 18, 21.

66   Ibid., pp. 109–170.

67   United Nations Children's Fund, 'What's so special about UNICEF's approach to early childhood?', UNICEF, New York, (date not given), <www.unicef.org/earlychildhood/index_integratedapproach.html>, accessed 29 June 2007.

68   Committee on the Rights of the Child, 'General Comment No. 7: Implementing child rights in early childhood', CRC/C/GC7, 2005, para. 22.

69   Lansdown, Gerison, *Disabled Children in Nepal: Progress in implementing the Convention on the Rights of the Child*, Rights for Disabled Children/Disability Awareness in Action, London, 2003, online at <www.daa.org.uk/RDC%20Nepal.htm>, accessed 10 July 2007.

70   United Nations Children's Fund, 'Children as Community Researchers', UNICEF, last revised March 2001, p. 30, online at <www.unicef.org/teachers/researchers/>, accessed 29 June 2007.

71   United Nations Children's Fund, *The State of the World's Children 2004: Girls, education and development*, UNICEF, New York, 2003, p. 87.

72   For more details on community learning centres, see UNESCO Bangkok, <www.unescobk.org/index.php?id=220/index.htm>, accessed 29 June 2007.

73   See, for example, Pigozzi, Mary Joy, 'Education for Emergencies and for Reconstruction: A developmental approach', United Nations Children's Fund, New York, 1999; and United Nations Children's Fund, 'Building Back Better: A 12-month update on UNICEF's work to rebuild children's lives and restore hope since the tsunami', UNICEF, New York, December 2005, <www.unicef.org/publications/files/TSUNAMI_eBOOK.pdf> (available only electronically), accessed 29 June 2007.

74   For more information on the Inter-Agency Network for Education in Emergencies, see <www.ineesite.org>.

75   Frankovits, op. cit., pp. 50–51.

76   Commission on Human Rights, 'Progress report of the Special Rapporteur on the right to education, Katarina Tomaševski, submitted in accordance with resolution 1999/25, E/CN.4/2000/6, 1 February 2000, paras. 45–55.

77   World Bank, 'School Fees: A roadblock to Education for All', *Education Notes*, World Bank, Washington, D.C., August 2004, p. 2, <www1.worldbank.org/education/pdf/EdNotes_Userfee_3.pdf>, accessed 29 June 2007.

[78]   Kattan, Raja Bentaouet, 'Implementation of Free Basic Education Policy', *Education Working Paper Series No. 7*, World Bank, Washington, D.C., December 2006, pp. 21–22.

[79]   Ibid., pp. 34–37.

[80]   Ibid., pp. 45–54.

[81]   Save the Children, HelpAge International and Institute of Development Studies, 'Making Cash Count: Lessons from cash transfer schemes in east and southern Africa for supporting the most vulnerable children and households', Save the Children, HelpAge International and IDS, 2005, p. 38.

[82]   Meng, Xin, and Jim Ryan, 'Does a Food for Education Program Affect School Outcomes? The Bangladesh case', IZA Discussion Paper 2557, January 2007, p. 8, <http://ssrn.com/abstract=958723> accessed 11 July 2007.

[83]   Gertler, Paul, 'The Impact of Conditional Cash Transfers on Human Development Outcomes: A review of the evidence from PROGRESA in Mexico and some implications for South and southern Africa', Southern African Regional Poverty Network, 2005, p. 2.

[84]   Ibid.

[85]   United Nations Convention on the Rights of the Child, article 32.

[86]   Bicego, George, Shea Rutstein, and Kiersten Johnson, 'Dimensions of the Emerging Orphan Crisis in Sub-Saharan Africa', *Social Science and Medicine,* vol. 56, no. 6, March, 2003, cited in United Nations Department of Economic and Social Affairs/Population Division, *The Impact of AIDS,* United Nations, New York, 2004, p. 72.

[87]   Tomaševski, Katerina, *Human Rights in Education as Prerequisite for Human Rights Education,* Right to Education Primers No. 4, Raoul Wallenberg Institute/Swedish International Development Cooperation Agency, Stockholm, 2001.

[88]   Committee on the Rights of the Child, 'General Comment No. 1: The aims of education, article 29 (1) (2001)', CRC/GC/2001/1, 2001, para. 9.

[89]   Tomaševski, Katarina, *Manual on Rights-Based Education*, op. cit., p. 27.

[90]   Lansdown Gerison, *The Evolving Capacities of the Child*, UNICEF Innocenti Research Centre, Florence, 2005, p. ix.

[91]   This has consistently been found in evaluations of individual initiatives. See, for example, United States Department of Education Office of Safe and Drug-Free Schools, 'Peer Mentoring and Academic Success', *Mentoring Fact Sheet No. 7*, December 2005.

[92]   See <www.unescobkk.org/fileadmin/user_upload/appeal/IE/Publications_and_reports/Understanding_needs.pdf>.

[93]   International Labour Organization/United Nations Economic, Social and Cultural Organization, 'Recommendation Concerning the Status of Teachers', adopted by the Special Intergovernmental Conference on the Status of Teachers, Paris, 5 October 1966.

[94]   Chaudhury, Nazmul, et al., 'Missing in Action: Teacher and health worker absence in developing countries', *Journal of Economic Perspectives,* vol. 20, no. 1, 2006, pp. 91–116.

[95]   Wright, Cream, 'The Third Wave: When schools must be for much more than learning and teaching, *UNGEI Forum*, vol. 6, no. 1, March 2006, p. 16.

[96]   United Nations Children's Fund, *The State of the World's Children 2004: Girls, education and development*, UNICEF, New York, 2003, p. 78.

97   United Nations, 'Plan of Action, World Programme for Human Rights Education, First Phase', Office of the United Nations High Commissioner for Human Rights, Geneva, and United Nations Educational, Scientific and Cultural Organization, Paris, para. 18, pp. 18–19.

98   Seel, Amanda, 'Progress on EFA in Laos', paper commissioned for the *EFA Global Monitoring Report 2003/4: The leap to equality*, United Nations Educational, Scientific and Cultural Organization, 2004/ED/EFA/MRT/PI/67, 2003, pp. 1, 5.

99   United Nations Educational, Scientific and Cultural Organization, *Education in a Multilingual World*, Education Position Paper, UNESCO, Paris, 2003, p. 7.

100   United Nations Educational, Scientific and Cultural Organization, *EFA Global Monitoring Report 2006: Literacy for life*, UNESCO, Paris, 2005, p. 216.

101   Dutcher, Nadine, *Expanding Opportunity in Linguistically Diverse Societies*, 2nd ed., Center for Applied Linguistics, Washington, D.C., 2004, pp. 11, 27.

102   United Nations Children's Fund, *The State of the World's Children 2004: Girls, education and development*, UNICEF, New York, 2003, p. 85.

103   Article 24(3).

104   Convention on the Rights of the Child, article 30; Committee on Economic, Social and Cultural Rights, 'General Comment No. 13: The right to education (article 13)', E/C.12/1999/10, December 1999, paras. 28, 29, 30; Convention against Discrimination in Education, article 5(c).

105   See United Nations Educational, Cultural and Scientific Organization, 'Guidelines on Intercultural Education', UNESCO, Paris, 2006, which takes into consideration the main standard-setting instruments that deal with this issue.

106   United Nations, 'Committee on the Rights of the Child, Forty-fourth session, Summary record of the 1219th meeting: Third periodic report of Chile (continued)', CRC/C/SR.1219, 20 February 2007.

107   Pinheiro, op. cit., p. 116.

108   Harper, Kate, et al., *Ending Physical and Humiliating Punishment of Children: Manual for action*, Save the Children, 2005, pp. 44–91.

109   UNESCO Culture of Peace Programme, 'Guidelines for a Plan of Action for the UNESCO Interregional Project for a Culture of Peace and Non-Violence in Educational Institutions', International Forum on Education for Non-Violence, Sintra, Portugal, 22 May 1996.

110   Pinheiro, op. cit., pp. 153–156.

111   United Nations Children's Fund, 'Strategies for Girls' Education', UNICEF, New York, May 2004, pp. 5–6.

112   Wright, Cream, 'HRBAP in Education: Global perspectives, challenges and options', draft paper for Second UNICEF Global Consultation on Human Rights-Based Approaches to Programming, Quito, September 2003, p. 8.

113   The right of adults to education should not simply be defined as an instrumental goal for the furtherance of children's education, but this wider entitlement is outside the remit of this framework.

114   International Labour Organization/United Nations Educational, Scientific and Cultural Organization, 'Recommendation Concerning the Status of Teachers', adopted by the Special Intergovernmental Conference on the Status of Teachers, Paris, 5 October 1966, Section VIII.

[115]  United Nations Children's Fund, *The State of the World's Children 1999: Education*, UNICEF, New York, 1998, p. 37.

[116]  Lansdown, Gerison, 'Promoting Children's Participation in Democratic Decision-Making', *Innocenti Insight No. 6*, UNICEF Innocenti Research Centre, Florence, 2001, p. 26.

[117]  Ibid., p. 5.

[118]  Bissell, Susan L., 'Earning and Learning: Tensions and compatibility', in Burns H. Weston, ed., *Child Labor and Human Rights: Making children matter*, Lynne Rienner Publishers, Boulder, CO, 2005, p. 389.

[119]  High Level Forum on Joint Progress Toward Enhanced Aid Effectiveness, 'Paris Declaration on Aid Effectiveness: Ownership, harmonisation, alignment, results and mutual accountability', Paris, 2005.

[120]  Organisation for Economic Co-operation and Development/Development Co-operation Directorate, *Integrating Human Rights into Development: Donor approaches, experiences and challenges*, The Development Dimension series, OECD, Paris, June 2006, pp. 69–89.

[121]  United Nations Children' Fund, 'Thematic Report on Girls' Education: Analysis of issues, challenges and achievements in 2004', UNICEF, New York, July 2005, p. 31.

[122]  High Level Forum on Joint Progress Toward Enhanced Aid Effectiveness, 'Paris Declaration on Aid Effectiveness: Ownership, harmonisation, alignment, results and mutual accountability', Paris, 2005, para. 3(v).

[123]  Attachment 1, Report by 'The Second Interagency Workshop on Implementing a Human Rights-based Approach in the Context of UN Reform', Stamford, USA, 5–7 May 2003.

[124]  *See* 'Plan of Action, World Programme for Human Rights Education, First Phase', pp. 37–51, <http://unesdoc.unesco.org/images/0014/001478/147853e.pdf>.